A TALE OF THESE CONTEMPTIBLE SUICIDES

Richard D France

First published in Great Britain in 2017 by
DeafNoise Foundation

This 2nd Edition published in 2019

Copyright ©2019 Richard D France

The right of Richard D France to be identified as the Author of the Work has been asserted by him in accordance with the Copyright, Designs and Patents Act 1988.

All rights reserved. Apart from any use permitted under UK copyright law, no part of this publication may be reproduced, stored in a retrieval system, or transmitted, in any form or by any means without the prior written permission of the publisher, not be otherwise circulated in any form of binding or cover other than that in which it is published and without a similar condition being imposed on the subsequent purchaser.

A CIP catalogue record for this title is available from the British Library.

The publishers would like to thank Stacey Communications for their help and assistance in the publication of this book. Thanks to Lynn Jackson for proofreading.

ISBN 978-1-999208-1-7

Cover Art by Mark Bushell
Printed and bound by Book Printing UK, Peterborough, UK.

DeafNoise Foundation
DeafNoiseUK
No: 159
2 London Bridge Walk
London SE1 2SX

E: deafnoiseuk@gmail.com

A Tale Of These Contemptible Suicides

Contents

One: Falling Without Realisation   1
Two: Sinking Back to Sheffield   46
Three: Moving On, But Sinking   79
Four: Sinking Below Again   102
Five: Up The Mountains of Spain   110
Six: The Lure of London   126
Seven: The River Thames Calls Me   130

Richard D France

1. Falling Without Realisation

I'm a mean mutherfucker from outer space and I don't want you blocking my space at the bar. I don't give a fuck about your opinions because at the end of the night I'll fuck up your mind. It never fails, and so far I'm still alive cos I've fucked up a few mean motherfuckers. I drink like a fish and I smoke worse than a cokeyhole, but don't worry if you don't understand that cos I come from Sheffield which made me what I am.

I went to the infamous Limit nightclub when I was fifteen where all the Punks, Goths, Skinheads and Rastafarians went tooting the old magic cigarettes and when it ran out I sneaked off to the Rebels nightclub where the Hells Angels and the Druids would hang out. In the daytime I went to the pubs where no one would dare to go to challenge those fuckers with my gobby mouth and I didn't give a fuck because no matter what happened Hell would always pervade their minds once I gave them a good talking to. Don't fuck me around cos I'll really fuck your mind up. And why not?

Basically, I didn't give a fuck until I moved to Oxford. What a bitch that was to be at the tender age of twenty-three and a proper fuck up that was what with all the hooray henrys (no capital letters for them stinky shits) cos they're a proper dick. I dragged the city to its dogshitted heels in my mind and no one could deal with my degeneration but that was my badge. I'm hardcore and no one wants to know me because no one can drink twenty-two pints a night alongside me and keep up with the viciousness of my mind that spilled its toxic brew of this obviously pretentious shithole calling itself the centre of the universe. For sure, there were the dicks that had the silver to buy all the champagne and jump the queue at the bar but they sure were flummoxed when they met me standing my very fucking firm ground in my paraboots and I always made sure I got served before them too. Lovely to see them get confused in realisation that money didn't always make the difference. Stinky shits.

Nothing wrong with stinky Oxford except my resentment as there are some people who are genuine especially those living up the Cowley Road, but such hypocrites when you realise what their aspirations are and always on a slimy, greasy pole. No wonder their girlfriends always insisted on drinking Pimms with cucumber and riding antique butchers' bicycles because they don't have time to explore what exactly their fannies can do until the next rich toyboy comes into town. Then they get fucked.

I was a driver in borrowed cars from the nurses of the John Radcliffe Hospital who were easily misled in my spittle of stolen words. I could charm them easily, leaving them with words of assurance that their well-earned babies of four rubberised trundling tarmac trawlers would be looked after, only leaving them with a hefty garage bill for replacement tyres and vaporised petrol afterwards. What they never knew was the stolen joy in driving dealers around the town of this shithole of bullshit intelligence, way before the cheeky joyriders started riding in stolen Maestros, the city of crappy Rovers and financial division, where guns were flashed and one hundred miles an hour trippy rides were had. Everything was starting to become a blur cos everything was getting faster and faster.

At this stupid tender age of bloody twenty-three, I was starting to want to die. I was rubbing everybody's noses in their own shitty minds. I was degrading all I could see. Everything is shit and life is shit. Work is shit and the bosses at work are all a bunch of wankers except my manager cos she ain't got no dick. I dunno. I was starting to lose the plot cos everyone around me wanted houses, career and aspirations to be better than they really were. What's that all about? I wanted to be with my deadbeat gang, while in the daytime I had to be with the conventional crowd. Money sells so I had to fit in with the conformity of the machine. Maybe I was naïve, maybe I was young but I could feel a growing sense of unease. This is not my machine to ride.

Drinking became my escape and smoking shit was my comfort, especially at the hour of bloody five o'clock then I would go find the glue sniffers and the outcasts cos they knew my language and I could be at ease, but I never bought the bastards a drink cos all drink is mine alone. No one gets a free ride out of me and in any case I'll fuck up your mind. Live at your peril if you want my company.
I'm getting angry and getting angrier every day. I can't live with this parallel of living by my hippy rules and working with the conventional crowd, especially not with the intelligentsia! They breathe words from a dictionary like feathers from a plucked chicken and it made no sense to me. I wanted to discuss Ginsberg, Thompson and Bukowski but

felt lost in their brief coffee-making conversations in the hokey kitchen, but it was no fault of theirs because they came from a different planet to mine. It wasn't their fault that they couldn't understand the merits of moshing to Lawnmower Death with its dancing rituals and charm that always made me smile while at this twisted sense of reality I didn't realise how blind I was to the refinery of cultural differences.

I'm becoming sick of the dogma and the rituals of the in and out crowds, of how different the hobnob people were with their sense of traditions as well as with the heavy metal crowd who simply were different to these mean motherfuckers I knew so well in Sheffield. Fucking Oxford! And to make it worse it was always crowded with square day-trippers from all over the world. Maybe it was my distorted reality of the world, but all I knew was sex, drugs and alcohol. Oxford at that time was the wrong place at the wrong time for me but I wasn't to know that until far later in life.

At some point I came to realise I was becoming aggressive with everyone I encountered, even my managers at work were becoming concerned. I was rolling spliffs at lunchtime and having liquid lunches where I would consume more alcohol than was reasonably acceptable and things started to get frayed at the edges of my life. People pissed me off and my girlfriend was pissing me off and her friends were pissing me off. Even the drug dealers were pissing me off and nothing held any fear in me except to piss even more people off. Not a good idea, but then I didn't care. I was becoming increasingly isolated and didn't have the rapport I had with my Limit crowd from Sheffield here because even those who deemed themselves the counter culture were always sprouting the latest in so-called alternative theories. To think that they could never mug a tramp for his alcohol was simply unthinkable to me, and to consider that such people would never consider bringing a heroin addict back home to jack up made me even more frustrated. What is this shithole of a city I lived and worked in if it couldn't countenance the alternative culture was simply plain unthinkable to me. Fucking Oxford. I was starting to realise that this is a city of haves and have-nots and I wanted no part of this bullshit, but sucked into it I was because I worked and lived here and had no other feasible alternative. I needed money to pay for my habits and the job paid well, but not only that there were some jewels in the people that worked there so there was some salvation in my self-inflicted torment. However, I didn't fit the dogmatic squares of their culture and conventionalism so it wouldn't be too long before conflict would arise as it did every evening in those lovely pubs of Oxford.

I'm spending more time travelling the city on my bicycle and going greater distances to find escape. A field in the middle of nowhere to lie on the grassy banks and smoke away in lost escapism. I was thinking of society and how different this place was to anywhere else I had lived in. There wasn't anything wrong with Oxford, it was my mind that couldn't accept its different ways. My mind started to deduce theories from newspapers, and I would drift into a stupor watching the traffic skim by. Work was becoming a dreaded daily routine, but as usual ended in the evenings scrambling someone's thoughts into mush, simply because I could. There was nothing wrong with meeting new people and then cackling into the night watching them walk away flummoxed at what I had just said. Language was in freefall and I didn't care.

I was getting angrier and aggressive. I was noticing certain people looking at me in certain ways. I was starting to think they were following me. I was getting a feeling of being watched. I consumed far more alcohol and drugs and while in this stupor I was increasingly isolating myself. A good friend of mine called Dr Dave came over to see me. He was American and a leading advocate in the fight to legalise marijuana so I always enjoyed listening to him and how he was taking legal steps to get cannabis accepted into the mainstream. He was an amazing guy and always had a dazzling array of different smokes with him so we would yak away into the night, sharing theories and conspiracy tales. Dr Dave noticed I had become somewhat 'distracted' and reckoned I was smoking too much weed. He gave me some black hash to rebalance my mind and this sent me reeling into a deep vortex of slipstreamed bedazzling thoughts. I was dropping fast into a pit of blackness and knew this was something different. The next morning, Dr Dave suggested I ease off a bit and get out of the city for a break but work beckoned and I had to earn a crust for my habit somehow.

Was I going mad? Should I have noticed the fall? When did I start to get paranoid? After an incident at work in which I tried to get some professors to discuss the merits of marijuana, my bosses were clearly concerned with me and suggested I go home and take a short term of leave. I wasn't too sure why this was, but clearly what I had just said was unacceptable. I know that now but back then, as an angry young man, I didn't give a fuck and I had just fucked myself up seriously bad. I walked home completely deranged and convinced that everyone knew about me from the way these wankers were staring at me. I noticed a guy following me so I took a diversion which meant I would end up following him and I could see I was making him very uncomfortable. I followed him to a pub where a group of men were standing outside and they were somewhat shocked to see me standing there, shouting at them demanding to see their IDs. I was seriously fucked up in the end but I didn't realise just how much. How strange this paranoia was to become.

I walked all the way home having felt that there were too many people on the buses who knew my business. I knew some shortcuts so I was home in no time unobserved. I guess all that training in the Army Cadets paid off as I felt safe, secure and away from any potential confrontations. I was getting angry. Why were my bosses at work being such arseholes? I stood in the flat above the shops watching the traffic and I was convinced that everyone was driving past to ensure I stayed at home. Right, that's it – I'm bolting the door and staying in! I found some sleeping pills and took 32 of them and fell into a stupor while smoking an extra-large joint. I was drifting into a sea of blackness where I felt some sense of an uneasy peace. This was better than putting up with the bullshit at work, especially with these wanky bosses in their fancy polyester suits. Oxford can go fuck itself but it wasn't quite finished with me yet.

I went to see the doctor as this rage was getting stronger and was referred to see a psychologist. I wasn't sure what this would achieve but maybe I was after more sleeping pills. Having spoken with the psychologist, he simply said to cut down on the drinking and get back to work. I wasn't sure what to make of this so I simply went home, smoked some more and slept ready for whatever the next day would bring. The next morning I woke and went to work but it was a bad idea as everyone in the office was gossiping about me and my manager called me into her office and said it was best if I went home to recover a bit more. Clearly the directors felt I had breached a serious etiquette in discussing marijuana with respectable clients and I don't blame them for this as it was of my own doing. I went back to my desk and gathered my stuff and walked home, again using diversionary tactics to ensure no one was following me. Such was my growing paranoia that I could only feel comfortable by staying at home but you can only do that for so long. Unbeknown to me, I was on a downward spiral to the tarry pits of hell while experiencing highs of glee and joy. I was depressed but didn't know this as I had no idea what mental health meant.

I took more pills one night, around 64 Temazepam with three bottles of wine and a fair number of joints. I was shutting down, blanking out everything. It was far easier to feel this way, to ignore the shit outside. The everyday world was not part of me anymore and people outside had all become my enemy. I was irrational with my thoughts, analysing everything that slipped past outside the flat window and not making sense to myself. However, I was experiencing a strong sense of spiritualism, my hippy roots were yearning to be free and yet here I was, trapped in this flat in crappy Oxford. I lost sense of reality and when I woke from this stupor I was blank in all sense of thought and feelings. I felt nothing. I could only think of one word and that was 'nihilist'. It suited me damned fine right there and then as there was nowhere else I could go with this shitty feeling my mind was seemingly dragging me down to. I was becoming a madman, a freak and an outcast. The outsider, the reject and the obscure. I was struggling with myself, struggling to find some sense of action that would bring in those beams of positivism I felt when I first moved to Oxford, and now everything was just simply morose and bleak.

My partner back then was increasingly concerned with my behaviour and tried to get me to get back into a sense of routine. I woke in the mornings and got ready for work as usual, catching the bus into town and then walking back to the flat. There was no point going back to work. Everyone was a hypocritical shithead. Hobnobs without the sugar. Dicks. Convinced that everyone walking in the streets knew about me, I would always revert to using diversionary tactics to sneakily get home so I could bolt the door and be safe. My mind tormented me about how useless I was and dragged me into a sea of stabbing sensations that left me feeling devoid.

There is no feeling like depression and even worse when you don't realise you've got depression. I had no idea about mental health as it was just another world that had nothing to do with me. It's something you read about in magazines or watch in a movie, nothing to do with me, and I'm convinced I'm fine but this awful nagging feeling was just a growing tumour in my mind.

With deceit or with good intentions, I was persuaded to get into the car so that my partner could take me for a drive to see Dr Dave. She knew that I trusted him more than I did her so it was the only way she could get me out of the flat. I sat in the car looking for secret cameras and not saying anything as obviously the car had been bugged. Paranoia plays great games and it always wins if you allow it to go too far. I was terrified of the drive, through the leafy suburbs of Oxford. We were driving towards Headington as apparently Dr Dave had business at the John Radcliffe Hospital so I was happy to transverse with grimaced teeth because with Dr Dave, you're safe from anyone.

The car took a right turn and we drove up a long driveway. I didn't know this place at all. I was uneasy straightaway. Warneford Hospital. No idea what this was but I was assured this was where Dr Dave was. It was a big old Victorian hospital with innocently-looking windows. Then we stopped. I didn't like this, I wanted out. Only then was I told that it was a psychiatric hospital and the words of Ken Kesey came flooding into my head at a hundred miles an hour and there was no way I was going in. There's nothing wrong with me, I'm fine, I'll just leave everyone alone and mind my own business thank you very much but no fucking way am I going in there! I was cajoled and persuaded to get out of the car; come, come, come see the nice man. He's a doctor and he only wants to help you. Such bullshit words, but life has a sharp edge to it if you're not careful to pay attention to what you're doing and I certainly had fucked myself up seriously bad to the extent that I didn't realise how much damage I was doing to myself.

We went into the cool interior of the building and were made to wait until the doctor was ready to see me. I was screaming inside my head to get the fuck out of here but yet at the same time I was so confused. I had taken so many drugs and smoked so much, as well as having drunk a lot, a goldfish would be seriously confused too with having drunk too much water! I was in a haze and in turmoil that I didn't really register what I was doing. My partner back then was really struggling to keep me in the building because I could be seriously unreasonable, but persist she did and stay I did too. Then it came. They called my name.

I went into the cool dark office of the psychiatrist and I completely lost it. I was sitting crouched on the chair wailing away while taking off my shoes. For what reason I still don't know to this day. All I know is that I seriously lost it and it was an easy decision for the psychiatrist to section me. He mentioned that he was surprised at how I was behaving because the previous psychologist I saw mentioned that he felt there was no concern for me except for my drinking. Was it then when I heard the deep cackling voice of my own paranoia laughing at me? Had I fallen so far down that I ended in this grim palace?

I'm uncertain of the conversations that took place in that meeting's encounter but as a result of it I was sectioned. Sectioned? Never heard of it! I felt utterly betrayed by these so-called people around me but nothing made sense anymore. It seems that my rejection of the conventional had led to this and I had to be reconfigured. Everything goes into a haze from here onwards. It turned out that I was suffering a dose of psychosis and what a marvellous new word for me to grapple with. Psychosis? Never heard of it but my mind repeated it like an endless mantra that it simply wouldn't go away. So madhouse it was for me from this point onwards.

I can't really remember if the nursing assistants came to take me to the ward or if the psychiatrist goaded me along or even if my then partner escorted me. It was a sobbing confusing wreck that dragged this sorry state to the ward to be introduced to what would become my home for the next few weeks. My room was a little confine of only about eight feet by four feet with bars on the windows. I just remember the wind that billowed as a teasing breeze upon my face. Shit! This is hell! I want out now! My mind is racing and I can't even motion myself to run. I'm trapped and have no state of mind to simply move. I'm crying like I've never cried before and this is what I've ended up in. I was given medication, of what I don't remember but it had a sedative effect on me and I became drowsy to everything around me. I'm feeling a warm sense of stupor and losing sense of everything that's going on around me. Maybe I slept, maybe I walked, but I don't know except acknowledging my paranoia which was shouting that this place was totally wired for film and sound.

I remember lying down on this infernal single bed that was cold and yet comforting, enveloping me in these hospital smells of an uncaring laundry. Prisoners probably washed these bedsheets for me, I thought. As I lay on the bed with the window open, a breeze billowed over my face drifting in smells of autumn leaves being burnt so I know it was around autumn when I was sectioned. My mind drifted while the travelling gypsies came to set up camp as I observed many pick-up trucks in the grounds, and far beyond reasonable description I could see that the Americans had settled into the distant building. Fucking paranoia, it really plays games with your mind. Even when I went to the toilet to pee, I couldn't because the smoke alarm was blinking its red LED indicator and that was a sign that the bastards were watching everything I did and do. Proper fuckers.

At some point I ventured out into the ward.I might have been called out to the evening meal and that's when I met them all. Crazies. Fuck that shit, I'm not one of them but there I was eating beside them. Food dished out ready served and they all ate at the same time. No choice but to eat what you're given even though there's a choice, but this was my first meal and my mind was absolutely bombed at this revelation. All these people were clearly from all walks of life, there was even one who played excellent classical music on the piano, but one thing all these people had was a look of a vacant stare. Shit! The bastards had put me in here with them and there was no way I was going to stay. I turned the fork over and over in my hand preparing for some form of attack but nothing happened except the motioning of these mulching mouths. There would be infrequent outbursts of tantrums and follow-on violence but this was quickly quelled by the ever-watching nursing staff. Crikey, on a grapevine, is this where I've really ended? The dustbin of society's rejects? Is this me for the rest of my life? I'm only 23 and I certainly have no intention of stopping here.

Everyone had a particular walk in which they would shuffle their feet. The medicated walk. The stupor of the fallen. It turned out that currency was tobacco and music as one patient had a really expensive record player with excellent speakers so we would all sit in the relaxation parlour listening to these records which could only be played if the owner agreed. It turned out that she was a heroin addict with a fucked up mind cos she had given away her children at birth and was unable to deal with the consequential emotions that would follow. Her partner had planted himself onto the ward as a voluntary patient so that he could keep an eye on her and manipulate those who were easily led under his control.

I'm not sure how many days passed but I quickly fell into the routine, even kicking off one incident during lunchtime when I was convinced that this whole set-up was a fake to catch me out so I threw my dinner against the wall and ran to the piano banging on those ivory keys. I wasn't sure what I was trying to achieve, but once sedated by the nurses and medicated I returned to the canteen to cheers from the other patients. What exactly for I wasn't sure but it clearly was some form of initiation that all patients had to go through to be accepted as one of 'them'. Through misleading conversations and mindboggling rationale, a dividing line grew the more one stayed on these wards of madness. It became a case of 'They', the nursing staff, and 'Us', the patients. This suited me absolutely fine because I was able to make sense of why I found it so hard to settle in Oxford. Oxford is a beautiful city heavily dominated by the Establishment and by those who wish to reach the higher echelons of society. I don't blame life for this dogma because everyone in life seeks to better themselves. I suppose having being brought up with the comforts of the counterculture society,I was struggling to accept this new way of life in moving to Oxford and seeking to better life for myself. In some ways I was naïve and perhaps unaware of the importance of having good connections and education while coming straight to Oxford after a lifetime living up in the North. Culture shock? Possibly so.

Heroin's partner was clearly the leader of the ward. He would control people including myself to undertake tasks he deemed necessary to maintain the power imbalance between patients and nursing staff. He was a clever man in the sense of mind manipulation as well as having a gift of the gab in that the nursing staff could direct no blame for any incidents to him. I would go for walks with him in the gardens of the hospital, picking up magic mushrooms and smoking toots with him that he somehow procured. We would often return to the ward completely stoned and dazed and then be forced to take extra medication on account of our irrational giggling. 'They' were becoming more awkward as I would have to see psychiatric students undertaking their university studies and flummox their minds with my words as it was so hard for me to accept that these young people could actually be responsible for making decisions on my treatment. I was returning to my old self of fucking up minds, but once it was sussed that I had been picking magic mushrooms from the grounds of the hospital I was given extra medication that floored my mind and the gardens were mown promptly.

Around this time my manager and three work colleagues came to visit me and I was surprised they would venture into a place like this. What the fuck do they want? Satisfaction at my complete degeneration? I wasn't sure what to do as we all were standing in the parlour surrounded by the other crazies. So I took them to my room for a little bit of privacy, but my room was small so it was very crowded with all us five in there. I mustn't derogate because it was nice of them to come visit, but what to say? Yes, I've smoked a lot of weed and fucked my head up? Or, no I don't think I can come back to work? We just stood there and exchanged pleasantries and they stayed for fifteen minutes then left. Little was I to know it would be the last time I would see such nice people.

It was a lively ward and despite my hesitation in accepting I had a mental health issue, despite my reluctance to come here, I had settled quite quickly with these odd beats of life. One game that was often played was Spin the Bottle. Whoever was selected had to roll a joint, which was risky as hell on a psychiatric ward. You could have your section order extended or be given extra medication. I've no idea what medication I was on but it sure sent me tripping up high to the clouds for a short period of euphoria then come bombing fast into the blackest of depression. One day that bottle pointed to me and there were about twenty of us in one dormitory sitting in a circle. I frantically rolled the given marijuana and tobacco into a decent joint with everyone sitting in a circle watching me in silence. It was doomed cos when the ward is emptied and all the patients are silenced then it won't be long before the troublesome 'They' come looking to see what's up, and they did. I was caught in mid-roll when all the nursing staff poured in, but wow, what a sight as all the patients would shuffle off taking no responsibility for this game and I had to deal with the consequences. I was taken back to my room and given extra medication and a telling off, then I had to lie on my bed while this shit stuff imbibed my head sending me to wherever my mind took me with extra doses of paranoia. It was an uneasy sleep that left my heart racing, but as soon as I recovered enough form the stupor of this I woke and raced upstairs to have a game of table tennis.

Around this time, a new patient came on the ward. She was a beautiful lady who was a ballet dancer and had been admitted by her parents due to her addiction to E's. Her long blonde hair bounced off her breasts every time we spoke to one another. Why we were attracted to each other I do not know but with the records being played louder in the parlour, we danced and danced and ate together, even eating the same morsels of food. She really was a lovely lady and I felt a lot of sensual emotions for her. Her parents would visit frequently and find us cuddled together, separating us with disgust, but we didn't care. Heroin's partner would observe us with relish and sometimes intervene if he felt her parents were being overtly unreasonable. Around this time, my paranoia was getting worse. It would take me days to convince my bowels to shit. I couldn't shit due to the smoke sensors but I knew 'They' were watching me shit. It was very off-putting but from time to time when the need to shit was so bad, I had no choice but to shit! As my paranoia grew, I watched the building across the grounds with the American flag every day. I came to realise that they wanted to experiment on me. I was to have a sex-change operation and become a secret agent in Russia. I have no idea where this came from but my anxiety grew every time I had to see the psychiatrist because I was convinced they would sign off the operation and that my dick would be chopped off. This went on for about two weeks until the ballerina told me she was a Russian agent and that it was her aim to save me.

Believe me, when you're on a psychiatric ward the conversations are fucking surreal. Everybody is in a surreal world of their own and when conversations are made your mind is taken on a long trip to somewhere in never-never land. Back to the ballerina who by then had convinced me she was a double agent and that the Russians knew of the American plan but that the gypsies would come save me. I told you it's surreal on these wards!

Anyway, as the day came closer to have the sex change operation, she told me that she would dance with me and tell her parents that I was the agent because her parents were working for the Americans but not to worry as the gypsies were waiting in the grounds. My mind's flying at a hundred thousand miles an hour trying to make sense of this, and all the while I'm playing even more table tennis at double speed trying to copy Bruce Lee because I know these skills will prove useful in the gigantic wars of the Americans and the Russians. What hope does a little Englander like me have unless I know how to attack with a ping pong ball!?

The day came when it was time for the operation and the ballerina was with me in the parlour dancing to another fine record because heroin mum was on a downer so she played doubly loud. For a day on the ward it couldn't get more surreal than this. As we were dancing, ballerina was becoming more infused with the sexiness of the music and become more intimate with me so we withdrew to my bedroom to kiss and carouse. We were rudely interrupted by the nursing staff who told us firmly that this was not permitted so we headed back into the parlour where there was an argument going off between some other patients. While this was happening, ballerina's parents turned up and were furious to find us kissing and caressing, which meant heroin addict's partner intervened and pulled out a playing card which we all knew meant we had to wear something yellow quickly. Such is the mind fuck of these wards that psychological games are being played on both sides, so about 20 patients disappeared to their rooms and dormitory to find something yellow to wear. This resulted in the nursing staff scrambling to find out what was going on, while heroin addict was arguing even louder and ballerina's parents were demanding to know what was going on. In the same instant, all 20 patients returned to the parlour wearing something yellow that led to more confusion with the nursing staff that was uncomfortable at this apparent show of force in yellow. I was told to stop kissing the ballerina while she was declaring her love for me to her furious parents, then frogmarched to my room and locked in until the chaos had died down. As a result of this upheaval, I was given a sedative and started to fall into a stupor but was visited by strange dreams. Someone with reassuring blonde hair was stroking my head and giving pleasures all over my body and it had to be a dream because my room was locked. When I woke in the morning, I looked to the chair next to my bed and found a pair of ballerina's socks on it. It's impossible! I jolted to the door to go find her but the door remained firmly locked! How?

At breakfast time, everyone was in a state of stupor because of the upheaval we had caused previously, so we were all eating extra bowls of cereal until it ran out then we would nominate someone to cause a fuss for extra cereal and cause a ruckus for the staff. Ballerina sat next to me and gave me a knowing smile and I knew it wasn't a dream that she had been in my room, but how had she got into a locked room? As the nursing staff were all in extra vigilant mood and observing us all, we couldn't talk as much as we normally did. I noticed ballerina's parents come onto the ward and when she left after breakfast I never saw her again. People come, people go.

I was given a stern talking to about my behaviour and somewhere around here my medication was increased so I would frequently fall into a stupor. I was becoming resentful as I wasn't allowed to go out as much as I wanted unless I had a member of staff with me. Considering the number of incidents that flared up on the ward daily, it's hardly surprising there was anyone to take me out. I had to go to the John Radcliffe Infirmary for a scan to assess whether I was suffering from schizophrenia, so a taxi was arranged and I enjoyed the ride from the comfort of the car. It was strange being driven through town and seeing the familiar sights again. The glue-sniffers were still in the same place and the masses throng of tourists still snapping away. One always saw the students everywhere, each with hopes and aspirations while I looked inward being a burned-out dope junkie. It's strange what perspective does when you've been locked up on the ward and cushioned from the everyday world outside. It's like a kaleidoscope of a hundred colours streaming into your eyes with unrelenting effort but this was it, reality, and it was exactly the same as the day I got taken into the madhouse.

I arrived at the John Radcliffe Infirmary and asked the taxi driver how I would get back to Warneford? He simply said I had to make my own way back and that set off my heart beating so fast. My mind was distracted from what I had to undergo at the hospital, only thinking about the masses on the streets that I would have to encounter and avoid. My mind was racing so far ahead that I wasn't sure where I was, I felt like running but to where? I had no keys to get back into the flat, and anyway that would be a bad place to go to considering if I was reported missing my partner would probably just send me back. Ahh yes, anxiety! What a beautiful word. Coupled with depression it leaves you falling so fast down an endless shaft. You know the bottom is coming but you don't know when. It's a hard ride and definitely not one for the uneasy. Brimstone and fire have nothing in comparison and burning in hell wasn't a realistic option right now.

I went into the cool interior of the infirmary, finding the right department, and ushered into a darkened room with a trolley bed. The nurses and doctors spoke gently and explained they had to stick some electronic pads on my head so they could record my brain waves. As I had long hair, I insisted on not cutting any off. Vanity stays even when you're down and out. Instructed to lie on the trolley, they shifted a lamp over my face and told me to gently relax. The room became even darker. Suddenly, a very bright strobe light started flashing right into my eyes and it was really strobing away. This went on for a good ten minutes before they turned it off. They were talking to me but I couldn't see anything, just shadows moving in the dark. After a few more minutes, they did it again and another long ten minutes of this seriously annoying strobe light was flashing my life away. Once completed, they simply said that the test for schizophrenia was over and that there was nothing to worry about. I felt like picking up the lamp and smashing it over their heads and flashing the fucker deep into their eyes, but imagination is a vicious thing if you let it roam free. I simply removed the monitoring pads from my head and they said I could go. I asked where to because I wasn't sure, but they confirmed that I was to go back to the Warneford and I had to make my own way back. Was this a joke? Or a test? My paranoia was a constant nag in my head. It wouldn't give me five minutes' respite.

I left the hospital knowing I had to go through town towards Headington, up the hill and then take a right near the Oxford Brookes University then I would be back in the safe confines of my room, safe with those bars on the window and with the mad howling crowd. As I stepped outside, the sun shone and my eyes were still flashing from the strobe treatment, it took a while to adjust so I had another cigarette, watching the multitude of students walking past the hospital entrance. My anxiety levels were rocketing as I knew it was time to shift. I had to get back but I had a flashbulb of an idea and decided to go see Social Services who were then based at the Oxford Deaf Centre. I managed to get there going along the numerous passageways, passing my old pub haunts and constantly monitoring people around me to ensure I wasn't being followed.

It's always busy in Oxford, a dense town with its population of students, hooray henrys and tourists. In that dark place of my mind, it was Dante's Inferno. I had to get out of here but I was getting closer to Oxford Deaf Centre and hopefully I would find respite.

As I arrived, I was met by a social worker and explained my situation. I begged for help and begged even more but it was to no avail. They simply wouldn't have anything to do with me. They just said to go back to the Warneford. I was dismayed, outcast and raging with filthy blackness. I don't understand social workers but more of that later as I'll come across them again and again. I walked out of the door and started making my way along the High Street towards

Magdalen Bridge when the impossible happened. I saw my crazies loitering outside a café near the University Church of St Mary the Virgin. They were all eating ice cream and laughing away. It's impossible considering I lived with these misfits on the ward and here they were so carefree and oblivious to everyone else passing them. Damn it! I knew it! It's a conspiracy to fuck up my mind. I knew Oxford is a breeding ground for the Intelligence Services but, crikey, to seriously fuck my head up this way? One of them saw me and waved me over, which made me even more fearful. There's no way that he can be waving and smiling at the same time. He's completely different on the ward especially when he's had his medication. I walked towards him then the others all looked and the sight of them all standing there eating ice cream was just too surreal to comprehend. I had to flee. I had to go. My mind was in complete meltdown so I just ran off and they laughed as I raced past them all. Complete traitors. Fucking nothing wrong with them. They're all stooges of the State, the Government and the rest of the conventional fucking squares. I don't remember much as I raced up St Clement's Street and felt a sense of peace and calm when I finally hit the boundary walls of the Warneford

Hospital. I was breathless, sweating and with a pulsating heart. I couldn't believe this. There would be no one in the hospital. Perhaps those damn pesky Americans were waiting inside to do the transgender operation. Where were the Russians? The gypsies? I couldn't see anyone and I ventured inside with trepidation.

It was lovely to be back inside, in the coolness of the building and the quietness of the ward was contradicting my sense of calm. There was no one around. A nurse came and asked if I was okay. I jabbered and shuddered looking for the bastards hiding in readiness to grab me and chop off my balls. Bastards, I'm feeling the sense to be very fucking defensive. Rage helps me out in these situations so I ventured further inside the confine. My bedroom was exactly the same. The parlour was empty so I asked the nurse where everyone was and she said they'd gone out for an afternoon walk. I'm not sure if I was relieved or my paranoia was building up, but then a scream came from the music room and it was heroin addict. She was arguing with her partner who amazingly was still on the ward. He never took any meds and ate with us all, keeping his shifty eyes on us at all times. They were both arguing about something so I went in and she calmed down asking me to sit next to her. I forgot about my intense paranoia within those few seconds.

She was bawling, trying to say something, then I was bawling with her. She was apologising to me because she didn't mean to give me away when I was a baby. Wait! What the fuck? Heroin's partner was hollering and shouting even more so the nursing staff came and pulled him away. There was a moment of silence except for her sobbing away. In between her sobbing bawls, she said that her family wouldn't let her keep me as a baby because of their gypsy traditions. She had been searching for me for a long time. She knew I would come to this place so she waited here for me to come. Her emotions were so wrecked at the guilt of this act that she became addicted to heroin to ease her pain. I couldn't believe this! No way! What about my parents? They brought me up and provided for me and gave me holidays. Why now? Why? She was crying away and I started sobbing as this was simply too confusing. Addict's partner came back into the room and started hollering away then the nursing staff came back and took both of them away. At the same time, the ice cream-munching crazies came back from their afternoon trip and were all hyper from too much sugar. Full of smiles and my mind wrecked, everything every day was simply too surreal.

Addict's partner came back into the room and he was angry. He accused me of upsetting his partner but someone intervened and said she was always making up stories. Then the nurses twigged what had happened and led me back to my room and consoled me. They told me that heroin addict was seriously disturbed and that I was to ignore everything she had told me. But what about the gypsies in the hospital grounds, I asked? Ahh yes them, they're the gardeners. Fucking paranoia! Always playing games and no fucking wonder I'm in the looney bin! I still couldn't shit properly in the loos because of those blinking smoke alarms, but it was getting easier especially if you sat in a certain way and kept your eyes fixated on the door. Don't look up when you're paranoid!!!!

Soon it was time for the evening meal where the latest gossip was about heroin's partner. He had been dismissed from the ward. Apparently, they reckoned that he was fine and didn't need any further treatment but he was banned from entering the ward again, even as a visitor. I'm not certain exactly why but apparently he was the source of heroin's demise and her downfall, but one thing we all mentioned in the parlour afterwards was how much more relaxing it was to be on the ward, in peace and in gentle contentment. We played records and were soon back to the giggling misfits plotting deeds and misdeeds against the nursing staff. Nothing ever happened but people would flip and do a crazy so we would giggle at this as the staff restrained such persons. Heroin addict promptly walked in and turned off her record player and declared that no one was to touch this, that is except me. She gave me a dazed look, obviously sedated to the hilt, touched my head and smiled then went back to her room. It's perplexing when something like this happens but you learn fast on psychiatric wards not to take everything seriously because if you do you're in trouble. For the rest of the night I got to play all the records I had wanted to listen to. Fuck the others if they don't like heavy metal and punk! Plenty of room to go hide on this ward.

My parents came to visit me but were very shocked and dismayed. They really didn't know what to do except to carry on as normal. There was no one in our family with a history of mental illness so this was a newfangled thing with sharp edges for them to wrestle without protective gloves. I was allowed to go on visits so my parents took me out and about round the beautiful Oxfordshire countryside but my mood was so morose that it was a struggle to have a conversation with them. They didn't do anything wrong, it was just they couldn't see how my mind was raging and the darkness I was sunk into. How to explain this if I had no concept of what this irksome loathing feeling was? All I knew was I was continuously sinking into some formidable quicksand in which the light was forever fading. I wanted so much to escape this feeling, to get back to my life and to move away from all this negativity. How? Back on the ward they would give me more medication and I had to see the psychiatric students who would ask me stupid questions and this was leaving me in an unjustifiable downward spiral. My parents didn't stay for long because I was festering with rage and in one incident the doctor came to insist on my taking medicine I was refusing. It resulted in six nursing staff trying to restrain me while I was spinning my father high above my head with my mother pleading with me to calm down. For no reason, something made me think of my friend whom I grew up with and everything was restored to serene peace. No sense, no rationale and no purpose because my mind was ping ponging all over the place and my energy was so high that I would frequently pop upstairs to the gym, exercising furiously then have a game of superfast table tennis.

One evening my partner came to see me while my parents were there triggering a rush of energy, so again I dashed upstairs and had a furious workout on the gym equipment then another game of superfast table tennis. This time it would be different as I felt my heart just beating so fast to a sudden stop and I blacked out and collapsed. When I came to, the emergency nursing team surrounded me and were in the process of starting CPR but luckily my partner was a nurse and understood what I was gesturing so everyone left me alone. I slowly got up and was escorted back to my room and it turned out to be mental exhaustion. Such claptrap I had never heard of but there you go; it's possible for the mind to burn itself out shutting down the physical side of my body. I wasn't sure what to make of this and my behaviour was becoming a little more erratic but I believe this was the side effects of the medication they were giving me. My mind continued to sink deeper and deeper into this black abyss of nothingness where to acknowledge it only brought despair and pain. Surely someone knew what this felt like and could do something about it but it was no good because they kept giving me more medication.

Things became blurry after this but I was increasingly volatile and erratic because the side effect of the medication was having a seriously negative impact on me. My mind continued to sink further and further into this seemingly endless abyss with no comfort to be found.
I'm not sure how it happened but I woke up in a different room. The view was different. The hospital was different. The door was locked. I had been transferred to a medium secure ward while sedated and was to remain locked in my room for a long while. Nursing staff came and went peering into the observation window of the door telling me to calm down and stay there. I didn't have a key and it was a formidable door so I guessed I wasn't going anywhere for a while. Night fell and I drifted in and out of drug-induced nightmares which went on forever before the rising sun of dawn.

After lunchtime, I was allowed out of my room and commanded to follow the nursing team. There were three of them escorting me and I was taken to a locked lounge with a huge observation window. I could see a fair number of patients in there all in a state of frenzy, but suddenly as they saw me enter the room everything went calm. The 'leader' of this room stood from his chair, the only chair in the room, and walked towards me. I was prepared for any necessary defensive actions but he simply looked me in the eyes, then gently held my arm and steered me towards this solo chair. The other patients were all stood in silence watching me and as soon as I was sat down (I was barefoot) they all started moaning, touching me, then lined up to take turns to kiss my feet. This was too surreal for me to understand but the nursing team who were observing this decided enough was enough and came back into the room, disrupting this ethereal scene and promptly escorted me back to my locked room. I was to remain there for a while until it was medication time and again fell into a sedated stupor. The very next morning when I woke I was back in my barred room at Warneford with a nurse sat next to me murmuring to me to remain calm and that everything was fine. Was this for real? "Hush, hush," intoned the nurse stroking my head, so I just lay there trying to make sense of this twisted reality. When I felt ready to move I got a cup of tea and went into the parlour, seeing my familiar inmates as well as a few new patients. They all welcomed me back and heroin addict smiled and put on another record. It's just another day down the asylum.

I was getting fed up with being here. I wanted to escape. My parents visited and I went out on a few trips with them around Oxford. It was nice getting out. I went on a day trip with the other patients in a minibus and we were taken to a farm. A proper farm, not the funny farm! As we arrived, I observed other visitors at the farm gathering their children and moving away from us as we walked round this place. The cows were mooing and the sheep were baaing, the wheat in the fields dancing on the billowing summer breeze. One patient was so fixated with the growing of sprouts stating she had never seen them grown before because "they usually grow on trees don't they?" We all went back to Warneford in a good mood and one played beautiful classical music on the piano. Dinner that night was extra splendid!

I was told over the next few days that I would be leaving to stay at my flat for a few days in the company of my father and my partner. I was looking forward to this but dreading it at the same time. What would I feel there? Will I be okay or will my mind run away again? My paranoia had not eased and this sinking into this black cesspit of my mind continued unabated. We undertook art therapy on the ward and I painted pictures of the supertrams being built in Sheffield, depicting scenes of machines devouring the beautiful South Yorkshire countryside. I guess it could have been a sign that I wanted to go home, to leave this city in which everything went wrong. To leave behind the darkness that had enveloped me here.

A few days had passed and my father arrived to take me back to the flat. It was nice to get out, but as soon as we got in the flat I became uneasy and restless. I couldn't relax. However, my father and my partner instilled a routine in which I was to have my meals and go for walks while relaxing at home. I couldn't step away from the window upstairs overlooking the streets below and felt everybody here knew me and knew me as a crazy. This wasn't acceptable to me and my poor father had to restrain and calm me down more than a few times. The only thing I hated was I was given new medication and this had a serious side effect on me. After the evening meal I would be given this tablet that my father insisted I had to take. He was only following doctor's orders so I don't blame him for trying his best. However, the side effect of this medication was the worst I had experienced so far. After ingesting, I would sit in my chair then feel a strange sensation come over me and collapse onto the floor in a fit. It felt like electricity was surging through my mind, through my head and throughout my body. I would shake in convulsions and it was extremely painful. I could feel my father and my partner restraining me, probably to ensure I didn't harm myself. It was so bad I thought death would be more comfortable. This awful surging, convulsive, electrical pulsing went on for about ten minutes, if somewhat ten minutes too long, and I would then wake in a dazed stupor. My mind was a tumbling numbness of nothing. I couldn't think while this pain was impounding away. This was grave, I thought to myself, and I had to repeat this shit every day for a few days, then it got too much.

My mum had come down later to visit at the flat but I was in a rage. I didn't want this medication. I hated this electricity frying my brains. Was this the chemical version of electro convulsive therapy

(ECT)? It sure was a bitch dealing with my raging mood every time the evening meal was ready because I knew what was coming and I couldn't do anything except ingest this dreadful pill. Each evening was the same routine and I fried on that grotty carpet of this shitty flat and I wanted out. I flipped into a rage so my parents decided I had to go back to the Warneford because this was something they couldn't control. As they managed to coax me into the car, my eyes shut tight at this mad raging crowd who were baying for my blood, the anger and the heat of their spittle I could feel. I was put onto the back seat while my father drove and my mum nursed me as best as she could. It was too much. Either I carry on with this shitty medication or I go back to the Warneford, so I attempted to eject myself out of the car by kicking the rear door open but my mum was quick to shut the door as my dad drove in desperation. I tried to claw my eyes out, such was the bitterness of this rage. It was better to be blinded than to see the shits every day that tormented my mind. Paranoia is a powerful weapon when used against oneself. My mum managed to prevent me from pulling out my eyes and soon we were back at the Warneford. The staff there were frustrated to see me back because I had become disruptive on the ward, so it was decided between the nursing team and my parents that I would be better off if we headed back to Sheffield. Pass on the shit, eh?

2. Sinking Back to Sheffield

It only took a couple of days for this to happen and I was soon on my way back to Sheffield. I was filled with trepidation as going back meant routine and following my parents' orders. There's nothing wrong with that and nothing wrong with their care and love. I'm a mean, fucked-up hippy who loves freedom but right now I have no choice and am incapable of looking after myself. Everything moved in a blur from here onwards. The doctors and nursing team were keen to see me go; perhaps I was too disruptive for them to control. I could fly wild whenever I desired and roamed freely deep inside my mind. However being on this cocktail of prescribed drugs meant I was still sinking. When would the bottom be reached and this feeling cease? Was it possible to fall so far beyond description? I'm still falling but it's all in slow motion and each drop brings an uneasiness that doesn't sit well and I couldn't rest easy knowing this was going somewhere I didn't want to be. Depression is a shitty feeling and I've yet to meet someone who knows exactly what this feels like, but I was only 23, surely I shouldn't be feeling this way? I was losing my sense of self, my identity and my sense of direction. It was like something was prising all my knowledge out of my head. My knowledge of aromatherapy was fading fast, and as my parents prepared me for my move back to Sheffield I lost my box of aromatherapy oils but right now nothing mattered except to get out of here.

People come and people go so there was no grand farewell in leaving the Warneford except a large paper bag filled with more shitty medication that my father carried. I'd have dumped it and run off if I could but it was too early to escape just yet and I didn't want to attract the wrong sort of attention just yet. I got into the car and we drove to the flat to gather my clothes and the few possessions I had, then left for Sheffield. This was the last time I would see my partner as a huge rift had developed between us. I knew I would no longer see her despite her insistence that she would see me in Sheffield, but I knew deep in my heart that I could never be with someone who betrayed me by having me sent to the psychiatric hospital in the first place. Trust is a fickle thing but when you're paranoid and making no sense, the best thing to do is trust absolutely no one.

We drove to Sheffield and it was pleasant to see the changing landscapes skim by. I was becoming more anxious because I would be staying with my parents. I had left home at the age of 17 to be free from their control and routine. I wanted out of the rat race in which I had spent a long 12 years in schooling and I wasn't just quite ready to go continue college and then drag myself through the gutter working away. It wasn't the brightest of plans but it was a good plan for me because I got to spend time with my friends and meeting the weirdos of life! Moving on, as we were getting closer to my parents' home, I was feeling very uneasy and sickly. I really didn't want to come back here. It was a shithole, which is why I left in the first place. I wanted to be all alone, but right now I wasn't capable of looking after myself and I had too many busybodies with the wrong interest in me. I had to see the psychiatrist and see a community psychiatric nurse and take medication and so on when really I just wanted to sleep and never wake up.

My paranoia and anxiety had got increasingly worse in that I couldn't venture outside for a walk alone. I had to be with either one of my parents or with someone, but alone I would fall into the cesspit of my broken mind and it was hard climbing back out of it. This black feeling was consuming me more and more and I was starting to suffer panic attacks because I didn't know how to deal with it. I was starting to resent being alive because if this was life, I wanted no part of it. I couldn't relax enough to watch TV, I couldn't read a book, I couldn't draw and I couldn't write. It was a barrage of uneasy, restless feelings where nausea would just overwhelm me. I wanted to die. That must be the first time I had consciously thought of death. Death was the way out of this morass of shittiness. How easy could it be? It was either this or continue with the routine that my parents had set up for me. They were only trying their best and had my interests at heart but I'm a freedom-loving hippy so it wasn't an easy adjustment to make.

I would read the newspapers, devouring stories about suicides, about deaths and murder. I could try murdering myself and this was a sensation that gave me a strange, warm feeling. It was an antidote to this awful falling nausea that dragged my mind further into this ever-increasing despair. My medication was strictly controlled and my parents always ensured there was someone at home as they had to go to work. Mornings were okay as I would have an hour or two to myself while my father ensured his shifts did not coincide with my mum's. It was difficult to have time alone and when I was alone I just stared into vacant space, tumbling downwards into this deep blackness that imposed itself upon me from nowhere. I tried to ease myself back into doing some creativity by dabbling in some graphic design but there was no joy, no pleasure and no imagination. It was becoming too much to handle. These newspapers were a source of information as I read more and more about people's suicide methods. Hanging was becoming a choice as it seemed a quick and guaranteed death. An overdose was highly unlikely because I couldn't access my medication, and anyway I reckoned I didn't have enough for a fatal dosage. I pored over the calendar on the wall in the kitchen in which my parents had written their shift patterns. There was a time slot where I would be alone for around five hours. This was enough for me and I started to plot. I smiled as I sensed an ending to this eternal torment on my mind. I would soon be freed from this dogma of routine and having to live a lie so it was going to be better for everyone once I had gone beyond the other side. I couldn't wait, as it would be another two weeks before I had those five hours to myself, so in this medicated stupor I just fell into a sleepy daze because it was better than having to acknowledge the conscious world.

It was a long time waiting for those two weeks to pass. Medication makes time go slow. A depressed heartbeat beats slower than normal. I am filled with trepidation because the days cannot past quickly enough. I am still sinking into this endless cesspit. It's impossible to sink so low but there it was, a huge invisible black hole that sucked me downwards perpetually. The day is coming and there is a sense of excitement but it is an uneasy excitement. I don't want to do this but I have to. I can't keep living like this, not with this black monster inside me. To live in constant torment with a nagging voice inside chattering away non-stop, I couldn't abide it for another minute. Thanks to some friends I had, they would give me a little bag of something to smoke, which eased up my vexed frustrations, and I would cadge a lift from my dad to go see another friend where we spent the afternoons drinking vodka. It was my way of escaping and it sure helped.

The day has arrived. I run downstairs into the kitchen to find an empty house.

As usual, my breakfast bowl has been laid out with the newspaper in readiness to entertain me. A cup of tea next to the kettle and bread by the toaster. Another normal fucking day but I was excited. I knew what was coming and I had to calm myself down as giddiness was overwhelming me. It was nice having the house to myself so I got dressed and went out to the garage with a dressing gown cord. This is what I had been reading about in the newspapers. No suicide note, as I didn't think it was necessary and I didn't want to jinx the deed.

I set up the stepladders and fixed a good noose, fastening it to the beam of the rafters. So this was it. A cold garage and my last view. I put the noose over my neck and tighten it, then step off the ladder. It was a sudden motion of suffocation and I shut my eyes as I winced at this pain. Everything went black.

The next thing I knew was how strange heaven looked. There were no clouds or angels playing their harps. There was no sun in paradise. It took me a while to realise that the coldness creeping through my skin was the concrete floor of the garage. I turned my head and found the cord still attached to the rafter, but that the noose had snapped. Hmm, how stupid of me not to think about my possibly being too heavy for a flimsy cord. This wasn't mentioned in the newspapers! Wait! How long had I been lying here? I got up quickly with a numbed mind acknowledging that I had tried to hang myself. It didn't register. It was just a task that had failed. I knew I had to hurry out of there because one of my parents would be back home, so I put the stepladders back and cleared the cord from the rafter, dumping it deep in the bin. I stepped back into the kitchen, put the kettle on and ate my breakfast as routine had me doing. It was about an hour before one of my parents came back, asking if I was okay and had I been okay in the house alone? I murmured that everything was fine and that I was going to go have a sleep. I went to bed because the medicine was still as shitty as ever and closed my eyes trying to make sense of what I had just done to myself.

It seems it didn't end here as I was back at the calendar, scouring dates for when both my parents would be away at work. It wasn't long before a date was found because this time, I had a better plan and it would succeed this time. In the garage, there was a rock climbing rope and this was going to allow me to go all the way from purgatory. What's to fail here? Days passed by slowly again and routine was a dreary chore. It's hard trying to live through day by day when you know the next day is going to be exactly the same. Time really does tick so slowly and a depressed mind is a very anxious one, coupled with increasing fraught at the thought of having to go outside.

My mother tried to coax me into going outside by arranging for me to meet her in town. All I had to do was get on the bus and get off at the agreed location and wait for her. This would help me build some confidence to go out and perhaps start making my path back into life. On the day of the deed, I opened the front door, saw a bus go past and shut the door, knowing there was no way I could venture out. My anxiety was so bad that I had no courage to travel outside alone and it wasn't for another two hours before my mother came home, frustrated because she was waiting for me and not knowing where I was. I was still sinking - and it's impossible to sink so deep but there it is – sucking me into this endless tormenting vortex. The deed cannot come quick enough and thoughts of suicide were so persistent that I could not think of anything else.

My father had sussed that I was smoking these funny cigarettes round the back of the garage so he sent me to the neighbour who was some psychiatric social worker. He was a lovely man and is still there so bless him for his advice. He told me that while he understood depression was a bitch to deal with, but smoking the old hoot in front of my family was a no-no so he suggested I carry on but be more discreet. The reason for this was because he had other clients who were going through depression but that quite a few found it relaxing smoking the old joe as opposed to ingesting the shitty medication the doctors would give. I often had thoughts of grabbing a doctor and forcing the bastard to take the medicine they were dishing out so they could understand the side effects of this shit. Maybe one day but maybe not, because I'm not a violent man.

Anyway, the day came when both my parents were out and I woke early knowing they both were out. I didn't even have a cup of tea, such was my eagerness to get into the garage. I hopped inside and shut the door with its familiar rattle. Here it was. My death. I couldn't wait because my mind was truly tormenting me. It was a fuck, because when I saw the psychiatrist they would ask if I was hearing voices but the answer was always a negation. I don't hear voices. I hear my mind chattering away. My thoughts tumble themselves into my consciousness. Isn't that the same for everybody? It didn't matter anymore because I had the climbing rope in my hands and I fastened a nice, nine-looped noose. I had practised this habit from the age of 17 so nooses were no problem to create. Perhaps I knew in my youth that this skill would come in useful but there's no point in regressing.

I stood on the stepladder, fasten the noose to the rafters and wound it around my neck. I tightened it as hard as I could, knowing from the last attempt that a good fucking noose would kill me. I was excited, almost delirious, knowing I was about to depart this shitty planet. Goodbye, every-fucking-one, cos I really am done.

As I stood on the ladder, I took a last breath then I jumped.

The pain was tremendous, I was really suffocating. My tongue really protruding. This is it. It's almost like having an erection but in the throat. I heard crash of the stepladders on the floor and hoped the neighbour wouldn't interfere. I was really hanging – this was it. I was blacking out and really struggling to breathe. The pain in my head was immense and everything was becoming blood red until I blacked out.

I'm not sure what happened next. I woke with a pain in my head and a distorted view. Was this heaven? Fucking rafters for stars? Son of a bitch! I struggled to open my eyes and moved to look upwards and found the unbelievable had happened. No way! It wasn't possible. Maybe this is hell but a confused version of it? As I looked to the rafters with the stepladders twisted in my legs, I could see the remains of the rope. It had snapped. A climbing rope? No way. While a thousand tumbling thoughts fell into my head at the same time, I was struck by a rising chorus of, "I can't die, I'm not meant to die!!"

As disappointed as I was that death had rejected me and that I wasn't deemed fit for dying, I knew I had to move fast. Mother would be coming home soon. I got up with a bad headache from my head hitting the concrete floor of the garage and removed the very tight noose from my neck. It's a bastard not being able to die especially when you're trying so hard. I really did want to die because my mind was so fucked up and that awful sinking feeling never ceased up. I don't want to endure any more of this. I just want to die. Something out there was telling me that I wasn't permitted to die and I wasn't going to get into an argument with God. No. Enough.

So I cleared up the debris in the garage and put the stepladders back in the same place, ran back into the kitchen and ate breakfast as usual so as to leave evidence of conformity. I looked in the mirror and had a red rope burn round my neck but it wasn't too bad looking like a rash. At least I still shaved everyday so maybe that's a good excuse which was proved when my mum came home. "What's that red mark round your neck?" she remarked when she came home, and rapidly I replied, "Shaving rash." She looked me in the eye and then made me a cup of tea and routine went on as normal. I can't fucking die. It's so unbelievable that I stopped reading the newspapers from that day. Fucking die? It's so damned hard but I wasn't giving up just yet.

I want to die, I want to die, I want to die. That's what I had to put up with every single fucking day. It went on and on and on. The medicine was really shitty. I don't know what it was but I do know two names: Sodium Valproate and Haloperidol. I had other medication but I don't remember their names. I was really fucked up on these and their side effects were really shitty. Fucking doctors, which is why I was becoming more aggressive towards them. It was a struggle for my father to make me go and see the doctors because I really would screw their heads up with my mental violence. My parents couldn't see what this shitty medication was doing to my head and I was still sinking into this black vortex, only this time I was constantly screaming inside. Screaming so much that I knew I had to die so it didn't take long to plot the next suicide.

My parents were really great carers even if I was resentful towards them. I don't blame their methods as mental health was something totally outside their realm. Hate was all I had festering inside and it was only because I hated myself so much. My parents did their best to instill a normality for me and I am grateful to them for their efforts, but don't forget I am a mean hippy and I will fight for my own freedom despite my misguided views towards them. It must have been so difficult for them that even now it's still hard to discuss the experiences I put them through. I love my mum and dad and I'm sorry that they had to put up with the shit I gave them but, hey, life is life, eh?

The calendar on the wall was devoured eagerly, planning and plotting the next suicide. I really didn't want to be here. I had to be gone. To be devoid. To be absent. To be null. It was a sickness to wake up every morning knowing I had to go through the breakfast routine again. My thoughts were so dark that it's impossible to write these down because otherwise you will be seriously disturbed at what I was actually thinking. Some things are best left alone like sleeping dogs.

It was around this time that I had to start seeing my community psychiatric nurse who was really wonderful. She was a bit of a hippy so understood my hostile cordiality. She was able to listen to my frustrations and give me guidance on what to do with my thoughts. A nice lady and I give her full credit for commitment to her profession. It's not often you meet someone who knows what they're talking about, especially when you're a paranoid psychotic. My sessions with her were a sense of serendipity and I found some peace talking with her. One hour with her was always over too quickly but whenever I left our session, she left me smiling so that was a good thing. It was around this time that a psychiatrist was finally confirmed for me. My father took me to the first session and I was actually looking forward to seeing this bastard. My mind was screwed and I was still sinking so I longed to lash out at an expert and see what they could do for me. We sat in the waiting room for ages then when I was called I was filled with anxiety because my father wanted to come with me. It was a tough call because it was the first time I managed to stand my ground with my lost confidence and say I wanted to be alone. When I saw the psychiatrist he was friendly and amicable. It was the first time I told anyone about my hanging myself. He was shocked to say the least but at least he knew I wasn't fucking around and asked if I wanted to go into hospital.

Fuck that shit cos Oxford had fucked up my head and hanging myself had screwed me even further. The medication was seriously pushing me over the edge and I really wanted out but I was in the game now with this psychiatrist. He gave me some other medication which for me was another no-no cos all the medication I had really screwed my head. I still had to deal with living with my parents' with their daily routine of Weetabix and porno owner's newspapers. I couldn't feel any emotions. Heaven wasn't willing to accept me prematurely and smoking so many cigarettes didn't give me the ending I so desired. Having convinced the psychiatrist that my parents were doing a great job of looking after me and that there was absolutely no need for them to know, he let me out of the consulting room having narrowly avoided being sent back to another psychiatric hospital and I went back to my parents' house.

However, a plot was forming as I had the opportunity to observe my parents. They always liked to ensure I had medication in the cupboard, even well in advance. This struck a light bulb in my head because I knew from observing the calendar that I would be alone soon with my father away on the night shift and my mother asleep at night. I am devious but then you have to be when your mind is dancing daily in hell. The devil makes no excuses in moments like this. I waited and waited knowing there was two months' worth of medication in the cupboard. That was the next plan. An overdose. It had to work. It was a serious amount of medicine to take and if one pill could fuck up my mind, then imagine what over one hundred could do. I couldn't wait, and yet again the days passed by slowly.

It was here. The day of the deed. My father would leave soon to begin his nightshift. Mother would sleep tightly as she always did especially after a bout of ironing. I was still sinking into the cesspit but I didn't care anymore because tonight it would end. The stupor would be finished. I ate eagerly but tempered myself, as I didn't want to make it obvious. I was wary that my parents would figure out that I was up to something. My heart beat faster that night because as soon as father left I knew I had to endure the night of my mother ironing watching trash TV then she would go to sleep. It took ages because the clocks ticked so slowly that night. Come on! It wouldn't tick fast enough for me. Fucking death. This time it would not cheat me.

Finally! Mother went to bed and I did my routine of watching drab TV then turned the lights off. I lay in my bed waiting for half an hour to be sure she was asleep. My heart was racing because I knew death was impending. Come on! I want to fucking die! Eventually, after time had passed and I felt it was safe to go downstairs without disturbing Mother, it was a moment of clarity feeling my feet descend the stairs in absolute silence. I entered the kitchen and turned on the extractor light; as this would not alert my mother I was prowling the house committing a misdeed. On opening the cupboard, there it was, a paper bag containing medicines that would take me to paradise. I was excited and yet hesitant because in all honesty it's not that easy facing death. There were about two hundred pills in total and it took a while emptying the blister packs. It was strange seeing all these pills. How the fuck was I going to digest them all? So I took them in handfuls with gulps of water. Swallowing and swallowing and swallowing until it was all gone.

I felt a serene sense of calm as I put the medicine packaging back in the cupboard, ensuring it looked exactly the same as how my parents had put it in there. Then I went to bed and lay down.

It took about half an hour before I could feel the first pangs of the overdose. I was feeling huge tingles of pain in my elbow joints. Then it reached my knees. I was convulsing. I controlled this because I didn't want to alert my mother in the next room. It was becoming very painful, almost electrical in its sensation. My body was reacting violently to this overdose yet my mind was controlling my reactions. I'm not sure what happened yet because after about fifteen minutes, I lost consciousness.

Everything is black. I am flying. Something hurts my head. Something is moving me. Everything is in unconsciousness. I don't care. I am dying. Maybe I am dead already. I do not know and I do not care.

All I know is that a conscious sense of blackness persisted. I remember movement but didn't register what it was. It was a long time in this black zone. I don't know. Was I dreaming? It didn't feel like a dream. Time passed I knew, but for how long I didn't know.

I woke and it was to the pointing finger of my mother who said, "You tried to kill yourself!" My father was there with a look of concern. My sisters were there and crying a little. I was hazy and I didn't give a fuck. I almost laughed but stifled it. Fucking hell! I can't die. I was in pain. My body ached and especially my back. My head was sore. I had woken at the Northern General Hospital in Sheffield. Doctors and nurses came by and went but I don't remember much. My family didn't stay for too long because they had their normal lives to live. I wasn't supposed to be here. Fuck! Why? Why am I denied access to paradise? Am I damned? I had a thousand questions racing through my head, but while I was here in this damned hospital I wanted to escape. It wasn't possible right now as I was seriously fucked. Apparently the flying sensation I had was my standing on the hospital bed and trying to fly only to hit my head on the hard lino floor. My mum had discovered me but not in the way I expected.

Fight or Flight is a condition of the mind. It does strange things when your body is put in extreme duress. Apparently that night after I had blacked out taking the overdose, sometime later, I walked into my mum's bedroom naked and threatened to set her alight with lighter fluid. My mother took action and phoned my father at work and somewhere in this mêlée I was taken to the Middlewood Hospital for emergency psychiatric treatment. The nursing team were seriously worried about my condition because I was not regaining consciousness and nor was I responding to their treatment. They informed my parents that it was looking like a 50/50 scenario in which I could possibly die. My parents were confused because the medication package at home was intact but they didn't realise it was empty until later. A lumbar puncture was ordered to find out what I had taken, hence being admitted to the Northern General Hospital.

After I woke I had been in a coma for ten days. No wonder my mind was taking me on a long dark trip. It's similar to dreaming but with no sense of direction and everything is dark in that comatose state. After a few days' treatment at the Northern General Hospital, a nurse came over from Middlewood Psychiatric Hospital and I was taken there by taxi in my pyjamas to stay for a while. The nursing staff there were nice and were overly concerned for me but only because they were the ones that gave me emergency treatment in a coma state.

Middlewood Hospital was set in the grounds of a much older established psychiatric hospital dating back to the Victorian times. The old buildings were boarded up and the grounds extensive. The ward was a mixed unit and I was admitted as a voluntary patient so I knew I would be able to go out and explore the grounds. There was even a padded cell on the ward and once I got to know the patients better we would have fun locking up an inmate in this cell and run off leaving them trying to attract the attention of the nursing team. It was a laid-back ward with separate dormitories for men and women, kind of dated from the 1970s. There was a good programme of occupational therapies which included basket weaving although with plastic reeds. I became very adept at this activity and loved it. I had talking therapy with a nurse called Kevin and he was a laid-back nurse so it was nice having chats with him. I don't remember the medication they were giving me but it was much calmer than all that shit I had been taking previously . Obviously, being on the ward meant one was supervised so it was reassuring in that way especially after the horrors of the Warneford Hospital. Maybe I had become more accepting of my own mental illness.

My friends all heard I was in Middlewood so would come over to visit me. It was nice seeing them all again after the isolation I experienced in Oxford. They would drag me off to the local pub and we would return to the hospital drunk. Naughty, but a nice feeling as it felt a sense of normality was returning. Kevin's talking therapy was very helpful in putting my sense of perspective around my illness in place. I was starting to realise that communication was the issue that led to my isolation. As I had become older, at the age of 23, I was experiencing more indirect discrimination at work. I wasn't promoted or given menial jobs. When I started working as a graphic designer at a publishing company in Oxford, other staff made derogatory remarks in that I should stick to cleaning the kitchen for them simply because I had previously worked as a cleaner at the John Radcliffe Hospital to pay for my private studies. This was a new experience for me and I was starting to realise that being deaf meant there are invisible barriers, especially around communication. Even when I went out to the pub, people had different accents and Oxford being the 'centre of the universe,' with all its universities and students from all over the world, meant it wasn't so easy to lipread everyone. There were others who had no time to communicate 'clearly' or repeat themselves so I had started to become unconsciously frustrated.

I have worked hard since the age of 15 working for rock and punk bands on the Sheffield scene doing this for four years. At 17 I was working at a printer's and did this for two years before deciding to go to college. My two sisters and mother were deaf while my father was hearing so communication was never an issue to consider because we went to the local deaf club on a regular basis and attended hearing social events. Nobody in my childhood had any issues with my deafness until I started working. With Kevin's chats it became clear that my frustrations were down to how the world communicated with people and deafness is a communication disability rather than a physical disability. I didn't see any issues with my deafness being a barrier except for the one contraption that causes so many problems, even today: the telephone. Even though I had access to a minicom, it was the attitude of those on the other end of the call that was negative. It was the first time I realised that my deafness was 'an impediment' to my production value. This really screwed my head up but with Kevin's help I was able to rationalise this thinking otherwise I would simply get angry. Why society was allowed to foster this attitude when I could use my hands to communicate with my deaf peers and my lips to communicate with my hearing peers? This question stayed in my head and was later to become an issue.

While at Middlewood Hospital I received visits from my family and they were of a calm nature, having walks in the grounds. At other times, the nursing team allowed me to wander around and one day I found an opening in the boarded-up windows of the old Victorian asylum and climbed inside. It was an amazing sensation exploring this huge old building with evidence of previous uses such as Beauty Rooms, Hairdressing and a Gymnasium. There was a safe in one of the offices and some old paperwork was still there so it was great reading this. I explored the entire building climbing up onto the roof and smoked a few roll-ups, watching the security team patrol the grounds. How I giggled at them with my extreme bird's-eye view.

One day an old mate from school came to visit me so we dumped his motorbike helmets in my wardrobe and went zooming around the grounds at a hundred miles an hour. It was an exhilarating feeling. Such freedom that reminded me of my old hippy days and it was a joy having time with him. I showed him around the old hospital and we sat on the roof smoking spliffs watching the security guards hunting for us. They never twigged we could see everything they were doing and when it was safe to do so we went back to his motorbike and rode back to the ward stoned and he went home. It was a peaceful afternoon sitting in the leisure room that day.

The patients were all a mixed bunch, of various ages. I didn't really have anyone that was a buddy. As usual, cigarettes were the currency of the ward. There were two elder brothers on the ward and one would simply go out for long walks wandering around Sheffield, only returning for the evening meal. He didn't talk to anyone but himself and after eating he would crouch on top of the dining table, staying in this position for over an hour before venturing off. He never spoke to anyone but his brother would always talk to him. One day this brother approached me in the dormitories and challenged me to explain why I was staring at him. I wasn't sure what he meant by this but suddenly he became aggressive and hit me in the face. He continued to throw punches but I quickly deflected these and threw him onto his bed and went immediately to the nursing station. I told them what had happened and he was confronted and it turned out that he had become paranoid about my staring at people when they were talking to me. He didn't realise I was deaf and had to lipread, so afterwards he apologised and said I should have told him I was deaf. I thought why should I?

I'm not deaf, I'm not a label, I'm a human being. This added to my thoughts on the question of the way society treated deaf people which I would discuss further in my talking therapies with Kevin.

My friends came to see me on a regular basis and one day we 'borrowed' a wheelchair and went roaming the grounds. We approached the old asylum but security must have been alerted because they suddenly came running after us. We bolted back to the ward and sat down panting, trying to be as innocent as we could. Security followed and confronted us but with a good excuse we fobbed them off and they were left arguing with the nursing team while we escaped to the pub.
It was Sunday lunchtime so the pub was really packed. My friends wheeled me into the pub and the landlord decided to open up the back room so that we could be comfortable because it was too crowded for "a disabled man in his chair." We had fun drinking pints in this quiet room and once the money ran out we left, but the wheelchair got stuck in the entrance so I got out of the chair to ease it out; however, the landlord came out at the same time and wasn't very amused! We ran back to the hospital giggling away and were confronted by the security

guards again, so I told my friends to leave while I dealt with them. After I gave them a good stern talking to with my twisted mind they never bothered me again, but the window into the asylum was reboarded so that was the end of my exploration there.

It was around this time that Kevin mentioned that it would be time for me to leave the hospital soon as I was making good progress. I was hesitant about this as I was reluctant to go back to my parents' house. There was nothing wrong with them but being a free spirit meant I cherished my freedom and would rather have somewhere of my own. Around the same time I came across a poster advertising Halfway Homes. This was a housing scheme with support workers. I liked the idea of this so it was arranged for me to have an interview with them. The workers from Halfway Homes were very pleasant and informative. They had a lot of activities including mountain bikes which we could borrow for the day. They also organised field trips including hiking trips, while the houses on offer included group sessions to ensure everyone staying in their properties resolved any issues arising with a key support worker provided. This was great as it would enable me to reconnect to society and help to rebuild my communication confidence that had been shattered by my experiences in Oxford.

It was arranged by Middlewood Hospital and Halfway Homes for me to have a room in one of their houses, but I had to be interviewed by the current residents to see if they accepted me. I was a little nervous when I attended the house first chosen for me as it was in Nether Edge, the very place where I was born. How strange to end up in the place I grew up in and was familiar with. I met up with another prospective tenant who turned out to be from the year below me at school. He remembered me well from the deaf unit and was a proper chatterbox. It turned out that his mental health issues were caused by his addiction to heroin and alcohol. We were duly interviewed by the tenants at the house with a key worker in attendance. About two weeks later I moved in.

How nice it was to have my own room, to have my possessions with me again, to play music as loud as I wanted and drink as much as I liked. To celebrate our moving in, we ventured down to the Broadfield pub where I had spent many nights when working on the music scene with my friends back then. We went into the pool room and drank copious amounts of alcohol, celebrating our freedom from the hospital regime. I bumped into an old mate there who asked me where the hell I had been. I told him I had been in the 'loony bin,' to which he was promptly shocked, then dismayed, and walked out of the pub. I never saw him again. Now I was starting to realise that people had an attitude towards those with mental illness and now I was one of 'them'.

Days passed by in a blurriness of summer days out on the mountain bikes. Heroin boy, as I'll call him, had a serious dope habit. Whenever we stopped somewhere in the amazing Peak District he would whip out his pipe and fill it with toot and toke away. This wasn't what I expected from people staying in halfway houses. He also had a serious drinking habit and would often be drunk in the living room. His choice, I thought. The team from Halfway Homes visited twice a week and all tenants had to go to head office once a week for a group meeting to discuss issues and activities. It was a really nice place to be involved with and made me more accepting of my own mental health. We were given housekeeping tasks on a rota basis so the houses were always clean which suited me fine. Heroin boy was smoking a lot more weed than was healthy for him. I recognised the signs of his addiction creeping back and knew he would fall sometime soon. Around this time I decided to go back to college to study for further qualifications as this would be an ideal stepping stone for me to return to work.

I studied chemistry, biology, physics and environmental science but I couldn't seem to retain the knowledge needed for the exams. Maybe it was the medication affecting me, or it was that the subjects were not suitable for me. I was very open about my mental health condition but this resulted in the other students on the course keeping a distance from me. I was learning more about attitudes and now I had attitudes towards deafness and mental health to deal with. I was also seeing a Community Psychiatric Nurse (CPN) and she was a really lovely lady who was also an old hippy so that made it easier for me to talk to her about any questions I had on my mind. Later, I decided that these subjects were not what I wanted to study as I was getting stressed trying to understand the complexities of the periodic table in chemistry and biology was just way beyond my comprehension. I swapped chemistry and biology to study politics and communications instead while keeping physics and environmental science. I thrived with this change of tack and my mind was more at ease. I wrote stories in communications that made me realise I liked to explore the dark side of humanity and soon came across nihilistic theories that really interested me. I completed my studies and heroin boy was becoming increasingly heavy with his drug habit. Around this time, I met a lady who would become my wife so I moved out and got on with life.

It had been about one year of living in the halfway house and it was really beneficial to me. Unfortunately, familiarity really does breed contempt and it wasn't long before relationships were becoming frayed in the house so I guess I left at the right time because I wanted to get back to work, get back to life and continue achieving to the best of my abilities. After a year of courting my girlfriend, we got married and moved to Coventry where I worked as a graphic designer in an art gallery and museum.

3. Moving On, But Sinking

I enjoyed this work and the staff there were wonderful. I experienced a moment of discrimination with my line manager as it turned out I wouldn't get promoted because I couldn't use the telephone, and my manager had found out about my mental health history to which he retorted that he would have never employed me if he had known. My wife was struggling to settle in Coventry because as a sculptor she found it hard to find an independent studio. She had worked with all the local steel companies back in Sheffield but Coventry had a different economy so it was harder for her to make the useful local links essential to her work. It was around this time that she was approached by social services to work with young people and she really loved this work, but it meant late hours especially if she was to engage with troubled youths on the streets. This had an impact on our relationship as she came home in the early hours of the mornings whereas I had to work regular hours. I was also attending Coventry Deaf Club where I enjoyed meeting people and signing away, but my wife was reluctant to become involved in this world.

I started studying psychology at the local college in the evenings but was dismayed when my line manager said he would study the same course. I studied for a year and when it was time for the exams I met my manager outside the hall, declaring I was going for a 'last cigarette' before starting. I walked out of the building and went home because I felt I wasn't ready and needed to study further. Needless to say, my manager took the exam and failed so this vexed our working relationship. Around this time his manager used to go outside with me for a cigarette and while chatting she hinted that it would be a good idea to go to university because there would be no promotion opportunities for me at work. I was increasingly unhappy at home because my wife was continuously working late hours. I was isolated again and soon the frustrations being to build up again. After chatting with my wife I decided to go to university in Hull and see how the relationship would pan out.

The first year at university passed quickly but in the second year my habit of smoking shit had returned. I was uneasy because my relationship with my wife was failing and we had agreed to divorce. It was strange at university because I started my studies at the age of

27 and I was surrounded by 18-year-old students who were obviously still babies in their parents' eyes. Their experiences of life could not match mine at 15 years old. Who goes drinking with the Hells Angels and Druids as well as the punks of Sheffield? I certainly had learnt a lot in my early years of adulthood and these bright-eyed innocent students were just discovering the joys of alcohol at this late tender age of 18. Once again I became isolated and started living life on my own outside university. I left the student digs quickly finding it wasn't for me and moved to Hessle Road in the west of the city where life certainly was far more interesting. I spent most of my time roaming the city on my bicycle, especially along the mighty River Humber. It's an amazing city but at that time was blighted by heroin. Getting divorced in the middle of my studies didn't leave me feeling good. I rode through the night returning to my flat around four in the morning then waking at six to go to university. I was the first at university and the last to leave as I would return there after the afternoon drinking session to chat to the Fine Art students who were more mature and intelligent to debate with. An 18-year-old getting excited about triple for single shots wasn't something I could empathise with and it

was around this time that the questions on my mind came back bothering me again.

I would travel the city with a bottle of brandy, riding as far as the Humber Bridge then going in the opposite direction along the river front to the ferry port and watch the ferries leave for Rotterdam. It's really an amazing place once you get to know the people there and such salt of the earth they are. They welcomed me into the local pubs and I sat with the locals chatting away about everything, which was far better than sitting in the rooms designated for students. My smoking habits increased so I rode stoned, drank brandy and then smoked some more before going back home. My mind was a rush of creative ideas for my studies as well as analysing life in detail that was similar to when I was in Oxford. I started debating with some of the lecturers at university, challenging their principles. This was healthy at the start as they liked debate, but then I would twist their words leaving them uncomfortable with a taste of bile in their own mouths. I wasn't a pleasant person then. I was a proper fuck-up but I loved it at university. I started debating with the Vice Principal, often storming into his office, and would debate away.

He found me a tough cookie to deal with but I had to push his ideals to the limit because university for me then should have been a place to encourage creativity but I was finding it becoming a factory fodder, churning out students in readiness for the workplace. Maybe it was my time I spent with Fine Art students who were really excellent with their theories; maybe I was overreaching myself with far-fetched ideas of what should be.

I started seeing another woman who was a heavy smoker so my smoking habit increased dramatically. This wasn't a good idea especially in the final year of my studies. I found her demanding as well as my having to commit to work as documentary producer for a local company in order to fund my studies. Suddenly the pressure ratcheted up and time was thin for everything that needed to be completed. The weekends would be spent with my girlfriend who liked to smoke a lot. The week was a plethora of my university studies and working part-time. My debates with the Vice Principle were increasing in their ferocity and we both became very stubborn in our arguments. My girlfriend was increasingly demanding and I was also dealing with the fallout of my recent divorce. Whenever I was home alone I would venture out on my bike at all hours. Freedom was always in the cold hours of the night. I had to move to East Hull as it was cheaper, but the people over there are different to those in West Hull. There is a rivalry between both sides but I found those on the East side more hostile to be with, possibly due to poverty and the affluence of heroin. I was soon targeted by kids because of my deafness and they would ring my doorbell throwing stones at me when I answered the door. All this didn't leave me feeling good and the question of my deafness arose again.

One day it all got too much and my parents realised this so they came over. My girlfriend was with me and she was too much for me. In the mess of this squabble that followed, I had enough. I told my father I needed him to phone an ambulance which he said wasn't necessary. I told my girlfriend to go home, which she refused. It all bubbled up to an explosive point where I grabbed hold of a corkscrew and threatened to stab it into my ear unless a fucking ambulance was called. Everyone froze when they realised I was being serious about harming myself. I didn't give a fuck anymore and I just needed people to start listening to me and start taking me seriously instead of this namby-pampy bullshit I was getting. The ambulance arrived but the crew were pissed off because they said there was nothing wrong with me. I knew the procedures to psychiatric hospitals and this was the way to do it. I was really fucking angry with everyone and eventually the crew agreed to take me to the hospital. I told them to strap me down in the stretcher because I knew my rage was coming back. They refused and I kicked off so they belted me down. On arrival at the hospital they put me into A&E to await an assessment from a doctor. This was taking a while and my father had come with me. I was seriously fucked off but after waiting a while I could feel the old paranoia coming back. Fuck this shit, I thought, and decided to leave. I decided a walk was far better than hanging around this awful sterile place. My father tried to restrain me from going but I shrugged him aside and started making my way towards the exit. I saw a security guard coming towards me and in my paranoia I stopped him and asked if he had powers of arrest. He replied negatively so I smiled with glee and carried on striding towards the exit. As I got outside my father pleaded with me to come back inside, but I smelled the sea air outside and knew where I wanted to go so I ran off into the dark night.

It was wonderful being so free. Nobody was hassling me and nobody was disagreeing with me. I was on my own and it was such a beautiful feeling. I found a recycling bin and dumping my passport into it left me feeling a high sense of euphoria. Now the Queen didn't owe me anymore! I slunk off pounding the streets of Hull, walking from the Hull Royal Infirmary all the way to Portobello Street in East Hull via the riverfront. It was such a long walk but it was such a wonderful sense of freedom walking these dark empty streets. I walked to my house but I didn't have any keys and there was nobody in so I carried on walking all the way back to St Andrew's Docks, venturing in the old docks that had filled in. I ran along the riverfront further up on the muddy shores and was covered head to toe in glorious mud. I was having so much fun that I forgot about time and suddenly dawn was rising. There was no way I could get home without attracting attention to my shrivelled state so I had no choice but to ring the non-emergency number for the police and leave the phone dangling in the call box in the hope the cops would send someone round to find me.

Sure enough a panda rolled up with a sole officer. He looked aghast when he saw me. I was covered head to toe in the glorious River Humber mud. I had been scrabbling over the old St Andrew's Docks, had a light show against the outline of the derelict Lord Line Building and frolicked along the banks of the River Humber. It was a sense of exhilaration being so free, doing whatever I wanted and chatting to the wondrous starlit skies. I wanted to stay here forever but rising dawn was telling me that the conventional time was coming.

It was here while I was jabbering to a bewildered police officer that I must have freaked him out because he refused to get out of the car, sitting there listening to my demands for cigarettes which he reluctantly gave. The peace was restored as I was ordered to sit on the wall while he made radio inquiries, his eyes never leaving mine. I was restless, hyper and bored. A dangerous combination, as I picked up a branch and put it in my ear and swirled it round like a searching antenna looking for a tune. The officer was bewildered even more and gestured angrily at me to stay where I was. I looked straight into his eyes with my wildest stare and mouthed to him that "I can hear everything." This was only edging me on as I knew he was more fearful of me than I was of him so I started jockeying around to his ever-increasing waggling finger and frantic shouting.

Luckily my father pulled up before this incident could get worse and was kind of pleased to see me but not surprised at how I looked. I had beaming eyes filled with the vitality of my night's sojourn and I felt so alive. My father wrapped me in a blanket and took me to hospital where I was put into a dank room with a number of chairs around. The nurse came along and gave me a cup of tea and told me to sit and wait. One by one, around seven members of the nursing team walked in, three of them psychiatrists. They all sat huddled round and started asking questions. I can't remember what these were but after getting bored of listening to them I decided to play a mind game with the slogan, "Show me the logo." This was a tag line from a tyre advertisement that really gripped me and I couldn't resist this tune. I played the game that is about illusions hidden in words and tried to influence their minds with thoughts.

I revealed a Union Jack emblem attached to my blanket and spun some yarn about how the Union Jack should always be presented when working in official roles, but if the tape is removed you'll see I'm

advertising a car! Then I started a rhapsody seeing this tag line over and over shouting, "Show me the logo!!!!"
Naturally the nursing team were dismayed realising I was simply out of control so a few words were said that I didn't catch, and the room emptied. They had sectioned me.

I waited a few more minutes in the presence of nursing staff with wary eyes, then two burly paramedics with full body armour and combat boots came to get me and escort me to the ambulance. They're the crew that deals with the Saturday night crowd so they don't mess about. I was escorted with both of them by my side, holding firmly onto my arms and bundled into the back of the ambulance. One stayed in the back with me and the other went to drive. I tried to ask questions about where they were taking me but the crew fingered me to be quiet. It was a very short ride. Probably the shortest or fastest ambulance trip I've ever had. I was in the ambulance for no longer than three minutes before it stopped and the rear doors were opened. There were more nursing staff who escorted me inside a low-slung anonymous building.

This new 'home' was a tricky one, especially with its security. All doors were locked and only staff had access. It was my first time in a segregated ward. There was a small garden with walls high enough to scale but this place was heavily staffed. I was put into the social room, being told to relax and watch TV. It was very early in the morning so the other patients hadn't woken yet. I was fuck-up wary of this place. It had a hostile feel to it. With all the doors locked, it had more of a prison feel. Reflected glass and windows that only opened a centimetre wide. This is a place designed to keep you inside. It wasn't long before I met my first inmate. He had a very violent and edgy manner. A proper nutcase considering how he was shouting at the staff already and breakfast hadn't been served yet.

The other patients came on the ward but there were only a few of them. Nutcase was striding round the room in circles seemingly casing me. I learn very quickly that he's the 'leader' of the ward and that his customary welcome is a Glaswegian Kiss. I didn't fancy that so I started getting defensive. Soon he swooped on me and pushed me to a chair, grappling with my neck, ready to head-butt me. His forehead was pressed hard against mine so I whispered, "I've done nothing wrong," over and over. He was in a rage then something twitched as I continued repeating myself, "I've done nothing wrong."

He seemingly lost his strength, looked at me and simply said, "I hear you," getting up and hauled me up beside him offering me a cigarette for 'before breakfast,' he said, winking.

Phew! I was so glad I didn't end with another broken nose that morning. This was a serious ward and plenty of shit going off. It's more aggressive on a male dominated ward. Apparently the females were in the next corridor but this segregated crap made it feel more like a prison. It turned out this place was called Miranda House.

I was seriously sectioned as I was not allowed to leave the hospital. The staff were not really around whenever there was trouble and there was plenty. Nutcase would threaten others for cigarettes and was easy with his punches. He was a hardcore muscular fighting machine. I got to know him better and it turned out he was a roofer. He was here because he'd recently separated and just lost it on a bender. There's a fine line between listening too much and knowing too much. He clearly was very pissed off but in the end he was in love and that had broken down.

I was pleased because the nursing team were insisting I be medicated. I refused and Nutcase would step in so giving me time and space to think what to do next. I was escorted to my room and given a stark choice, "Take the medicine or we inject you."

You know when you've got to play the game. I took the pills because good behaviour gets you out quicker than screwing up your chances of freedom. I was made to tell them what I had done with my passport and where all my belongings were. I went out with a member of the nursing team in their car to the recycling bin and what fun we had trying to fish out my passport. The State does not give up its own so easily, I thought. After returning to hospital it soon became a routine of sleep, eat, sleep, eat, TV, eat and sleep. Everything slows down here. Later that evening, when Sunday dinner was served, I didn't want to eat anything but the nursing staff was insisting, so I kicked off a little to test the temperature and told the patients that as it was Sunday I couldn't eat in the witness of the Lord without a prayer. Everyone put down their knives and forks at the same time and this alarmed the nursing staff. An alert must've been said as more staff came into the dining room. None of us would eat and, while I was debating with the nursing staff on the merits of fasting, I agreed in the end to consume a small pot of yogurt that was specially fetched. Now I knew what the temperament of these nursing staff was. Perhaps I was subconsciously planning a way out. As I spooned my yogurt I started whispering out words from an old Naval bible. The other patients looked startled and looked at Nutcase who simply smiled, stabbed his knife and fork into the meat on his plate saying, "Yes, we'll have that. Louder please, Richard!"

I resumed reading from the bible increasing the volume of my voice and I could see the nursing staff was getting edgy but it turned out it's always a bad idea to interrupt Nutcase's dinner. This lovely surreal setting continued into the night before the medication wiped me out and I was asleep. I had my parents visit and they brought me supplies. It was a bitchy feeling when waking in the morning to find all my supplies missing. I had been burgled while asleep in my ward room but the fucker at least left me one pack of tobacco. I knew immediately it was Nutcase but there's nothing that can be done because Nutcase is more useful as a friend than an enemy. I have seen the result of his punches on the ward. Make a choice.

As time went by it became clear that this hospital had some serious security. All entrances and exits are locked. I checked out the garden again but nobody is allowed in there without supervision. Hedging my bets, I decide to ask if I can go for a walk and to my surprise they said "yes", but with conditions. I was permitted to go out and walk but only if I came back before 9am the next morning. I'm a wild steed relishing this freedom and soon the city is mine to plough footprints. I walk alongside the riverside all the way to East Hull, all the way back to Portobello Road. I wanted to smell my house and I stood there with no keys, sniffing through the letterbox. I continue walking round the city through the night until dawn once again rose. I return with dismay to the hospital around 7am.

Without realising, my mania has kicked in and I'm demanding another walk. The joy of being outside is exciting compared to these dim fluorescent-lit corridors. The nursing team refuse my request and I'm starting to get mad. They insist I take an anti-psychotic which I refuse. I'm left fuming, pacing up and down the corridors. The staff is put on alert. Why am I pacing? It gives me time and space to think while keeping people at a distance. Also, while I'm pacing up and down the corridor, I'm also reading up on my rights on the ward because there is a poster explaining everything about the Mental Health Act. I'm learning fast, retaining this useful knowledge and scheming. I decide to phone the police via 999 and complain I am being held against my free will (worth a try) but end up immediately sectioned further so I'm even more pissed off. I'm still pacing the corridors, reading segment by segment of the Mental Health Act. Always plan on the next move as one can move faster and that's exactly what happened next.

A nurse had let herself onto the ward through the secure entrance and was momentarily distracted by someone talking to her from outside. I took this chance and ran towards the doors, gave her a gentle shove and flew down the corridors having memorised the escape route. I'm running free and the alarms are blaring. There are four male staff chasing me. I need more time for the exit so by sheer luck there was crates of tomatoes, mushrooms, eggs and bacon, all ready for the morning's breakfast. I picked up a tomato and threw it upwards in the air, mindful of criminal acts, and this gave me the time I needed. The first staff member suddenly stopped and all the other three cascaded into a sudden stop. Ha! I have an extra twenty seconds and I'm now at the main entrance which is now electronically locked. There's no time to pick up a chair and smash the doors, although doing that only leads to prison. Don't damage government property and never harm anyone, it will only make your own situation worse and you could be locked up for life.

I'm frenetically looking round my environment and it struck me I had on my blanket! This blanket has special meaning for me as it has now been to every psychiatric institution I've been to. I twisted the blanket into a rope and fasten the doors so no one could gain entrance into the building. My four chasers have caught up with me and I immediately go defensive, signing and shouting out the British Sign Language alphabet from A to Z over and over. This is enough to intimidate them to keeping a safe distance from me. It's great when you exaggerate this signed alphabet so that it can look aggressive to someone who can't sign. I could see more security personnel outside trying to open the doors. I saw a couple of police cars pull up but it was fine because my trusty blanket was guarding those doors. I persisted with my aggravated signing and shouting and there's more staff coming down but they don't touch me. I'm too hostile and demanding that someone to see me who can understand fucking sign language. Fuck you! Don't talk to me if you can't sign! Aggressive shouting punctuated by the interspersing of signed alphabet letters.

This is going on for long enough, about fifteen minutes, and I see more police personnel arriving so it's time to end the game, but for how long? Suddenly the staff withdraw and a psychiatrist arrives agreeing to learn the sign alphabet. He was shaking and frightened but of what? Me? I only stand my ground when I believe in something, and if you're wrong then you're plain damned wrong. I won't quit until the battle is over. I guess that mentality came from my time in the Army Cadets where the discipline there has contributed to my mental health survival. Anyway, I sign the whole alphabet from A to Z so fast and demand he repeats what I have just signed. He's shivering, a quivering wreck. He does A and I give him a menacing approval and immediately demand the next letter. I can see he's really struggling but appreciate the efforts he making here. He finally gets a B then I quit, take the blanket off the doors and go straight back to the ward with a lovely crowd of pissed off nursing staff. The situation was defused and I had to take medicine that calmed me down and went into the leisure room where my fellows were cheering, especially Nutcase.

I was happy even if I was sectioned for a further three months, but it was fine as my efforts in reading the Mental Health Act paid off with a barrister appointed to travel immediately from London. It was a relaxing day and I think that was the medicine. The next morning arrived and I was sitting in the leisure room slowly eating breakfast. Nutcase was with me and we were conversing about escape routes. The staff immediately came in and asked what we were up to. Naturally they kept a safe distance because both of us had proved disruptive on the ward, especially with Nutcase's propensity to physical violence. We both started mooing and baaing, two mad farm animals in the funny farm. The nurses were alarmed and called for others to come. They all approached us slowly demanding to know what we were doing. We were getting louder because every time we mooed or baaed the staff would take a step back.

"Talking about what we're having for breakfast with Richard," said Nutcase, with calmness and focused intent. I wasn't sure if he was serious about this larking we were creating, but the staff were satisfied enough to retreat to their nursing station and leave us alone. As they left and once we knew nobody could hear us we discussed these escape strategies some more. I learnt a lot from Nutcase even though he was a dangerous man to be with; we had a few hearty moments of long, deep conversations about life and it's surprising what you learn about wisdom, especially from people like Nutcase.

After breakfast I was taken to my appointment and met a very pleasant barrister. He had travelled all the way from London which impressed me, and we had a serious discussion about my situation and I took his advice accordingly. He went to have a discussion with the nursing team and afterwards they all changed their attitudes towards me, being more mindful and respective. He did a lot of 'behind-the-scene' work so things were changing again for me. How such minds have great influence in society.

The next 24 hours were a blur of activity as I was finally diagnosed as having the condition, hypomania. This is a bipolar disorder in which my mood stability is disturbed by high feelings of joy, laughter and hypertension, then followed by long, slow sinking days into the blackness. I was to leave the hospital and see about moving back to Sheffield. So passing on the buck again, are they? I was only too glad to leave including agreeing to take medication. It was during this time I met a trainee social worker on university work placement. She knew sign language and I was able to express freely what I had been feeling these long last few weeks. I was able to complain about how the system fucked me up because I can lipread and speak so was being treated in a mainstream psychiatric hospital instead of having specialist psychiatric treatment for people who use sign language. I was able to sort out my financial affairs in Hull by leaving my house. I was leaving Hull because my university had come to an agreement in which I was to leave immediately but with honours. I had to agree to their terms and conditions as well as inform my employer that I was unwell and would be leaving the city. It was a kaleidoscope of whirling emotions. I was sad to leave Hull, because outside my studies I really enjoyed meeting people here and their approach to life. Hull is a wonderful place and a jewel in these blighted landscapes of moribund.

4. Sinking Below Again

So there it was. I was en route back to Sheffield once again. I stayed at my parents but didn't hang around. I was well enough to go out and enjoy life although my communication confidence had taken a pounding. With the help of my then girlfriend I managed to find a flat with a garden so I was able to have a sense of freedom and, for myself, privacy to ride through the ravages of this depression. I didn't really settle well in Sheffield. It had changed. The flat was in an affluent area so I was mingling again with wealthy students that reminded me of Oxford. I would stay at friends rather than go home. The sense of isolation was creeping back in again. Despair knocking on the fragile walls of my mind. Everything is sinking again. Sinking into that relentless empty sense of blackness. Somewhere in this darkness, I took an overdose again.

I'm not sure what happened but apparently my parents were alerted by my non-responding so they gained entry into the flat and found me on my bed. I was taken to hospital and then referred to the Michael Carlisle Hospital again. This time I was on the Stanage Ward under suicide watch. It's a crappy but necessary routine. It's hard sleeping at nights in hospital as there's always something happening. On psychiatric wards there's always something happening but here nothing except the flicking on and off of the lights every twenty minutes to check I was still alive. A pain trying to sleep and just as you're about to nod off the lights come on again and again. I got used to this but the following morning I met my fellow inmates. They were all more civilised people with manners so I couldn't really engage with them. It was a peaceful ward with only the odd shout here and there, but very sedate in that I spend most of my time reading in my room and in the gardens. Time ticked somewhat slowly. The routine here was easy to understand. Breakfast followed by hanging around, followed by lunch then hanging around and finally dinner, then even more hanging around until it was time to sleep. It was dull but interesting because I wasn't medicated here. The nursing team would queue me up for medication then when it was my turn just say loudly and disapprovingly, "No medication for you."

I wasn't being given any leave to go out and explore the area. I grew up round here so I had plenty of places to go nearby. It wasn't to be and I remained under observation. After about a week of tedious boredom, and having read most of the books from the ward library, I was finally given leave but only during the daytime and supervised weekend leave. Tosswank. Better than nothing, I supposed. Soon the beers and smokes were flowing and I was spending longer amounts of time away from the hospital. When I returned one Sunday I was informed that I was to move to Burbage Ward. This was the adjacent ward and was more troublesome. I didn't mind too much as this ward was drab with the worst violence being a yell. I wasn't learning anything from the patients here so a move was good enough.

One can tell a ward by looking at the floor. Stanage was very clean, with polished floors and tidiness. Burbage was hell in comparison because the carpet was stained with numerous beer spillages, cigarette burns and a muckiness that belied its age. I was to go on the dormitories but objected to this as I am more prone to violence at night because I cannot hear anything. They agreed to give me a single room but immediately the other patients on the ward kicked off about this. The ward psycho decided to go lie in my room mentioning how much more comfortable he was there. This wasn't a good start. I had to leave the room while staff sorted him out so went for my lunch. The canteen was much different to Stanage, having its own kitchens prepare the meals, and was slop hell in comparison. I don't expect much from a mental health institution but we're human too and we like to eat with dignity too. The inpatients were more volatile, some clearly drunk or jacked up. There was more of a violent atmosphere here and there's always someone kicking off. I never sit with my back to these masses holding metal cutlery. There's no one to trust here. With my back facing the wall, my eyes eagerly scanned this inferno of broken minds. Never make eye contact here as they're a lot more unstable. As usual, fags were currency and the gardens had their places of sanctuary from prying staff.

I had more psychiatric team meetings with them always pushing the medication card. Every fucker in these meetings pushed me to medicate. I ignore them and escape to the park with supplies from Mr Pops. Soon after, I met my CPN who was another nice lady. She really listened to what I had to say and I was soon having talking therapy with her on a weekly basis. It was during this time that I was struggling with my then girlfriend and looking to end the relationship. She introduced me to a male colleague of hers who was happy to talk frankly, "as a man to a man" (his words) and what a meeting that was. We had a long hearty talk on the merits of masculinity and what it was to be a man in today's society. That really helped me put some order in my mind. Still unmedicated, I had weekends away and sneaky daytrips to the pub. Burbage Ward was very colourful. Always someone crying, someone suffering, someone shouting and, on occasions, someone fighting. Life certainly was very interesting and you couldn't escape for a bit of peace without another patient following you, always on the take for something.

Returning after a weekend's leave, I found my room occupied by an old hippy. He was a mean hippy too as he wouldn't let me collect my stuff from my wardrobe. The nursing team came to deal with this but this hippy insisted on seeing all their ID cards before any conversation could take place. I took an immediate liking to him and once he sussed me he introduced himself as 'Dave'. He took to trusting me as there's no one else out there to trust, he said, asking me questions about this hell that called itself

Burbage Ward. Dave wouldn't talk to anyone else and was wary as fuck. He was sharp with his eyes and never missed a beat of ward life. We struck up a close friendship as we traded roll-ups and became chat buddies. We had our routine in which we kept an eye on each other and met up in our garden space for a smoke. Dave was really crazy, a proper eccentric and a very strong character for a mean hippy. He knew what he was talking about apart from the giant lentils in the skies and how it would rain lentils on us all turning everyone into vegetarians. We always had a laugh and it turned out his sister had arranged his sectioning because she couldn't understand his hippy ways of life.

Watch out for the conventionalists, they're everywhere and they'll lock you up to get you conformed one way or other.

It was during this time one morning when I was in the gardens having my breakfast roll-up that this sinking feeling finally stopped. I was alone and still sinking, thinking that my future was bleak. It wouldn't look good for my career having a history of psychiatric hospitals. I was sinking and thinking that my future would be this daily hell imposed. Thud! It was sudden and came from nowhere. I actually physically felt the sensation of hitting rock bottom. There it was! Finally! The end of the downfall. I knew immediately that this was the end of my endless downward spiral. The sun shone at that moment and I knew I was going to be okay. It was the first smile I genuinely smiled with pleasure. Life was now on the up!

Time had passed and it was clear that the issue of being unmedicated was unusual. Other patients on the ward were asking me how I did it. One guy decided to refuse his mediation and ended forcibly medicated after smashing up his room in protest.
One day Dave and I were outside with the others, all of us chain-smoking and bored. Dave said something funny about the lentils again and I couldn't stop laughing away. I noticed a nurse exit the scene. The next day I was told I would be leaving as there was nothing wrong with me. I was sad to leave Dave behind and he simply said, "Hey, good to know you. We'll never meet again." It struck me deep when he said that because he was right. I went back to the flat and soon toot became my medication again despite being aware it was only fucking me up. However, during this time I explored music, having been introduced to a

music module at university. Time now was mine alone and I had a very creative time during this period releasing an EP. My relationship was fraying and my instincts were telling me to leave this place so I found a bedsit and moved out.

5. Up The Mountains of Spain

This was a time of rediscovery - to explore my interests, desires, career and pleasures. I still wasn't 100% but, on the way, there. I saw the TV coverage of the terrorist attacks on the USA through 9/11. This is all I remember about this time. One thing led to another and soon I was on a holiday break to Spain with my girlfriend. We had repaired wounds and decided a break would be good for us. I met some fantastic people and found a nice mountain to make friends with. I found it hard to sleep, preferring to wake at first light to go help pick carob beans for the local goats, and went on business trips in Marbella with an Arabic businessman. I was learning new skills and developed my understanding of Spanish language. I'm not certain how but in this mashing of opportunities and deals I'd bought a caravan and found a farmer willing to let me have a plot in exchange for labour. The relationship was fraying badly and fast. We were disagreeing with everything and I wanted to go my own way. I started hiding out up in the mountains, hiding from everyone. I was fed up. Was it all about communication or was it my poor handling of relationships? I heard there were some farm dogs causing problems up the mountain so I went and got my stick, a bicycle siren and a sliver of broken glass. I made a formidable weapon with all of these and as night fell I set out to confront these troublesome dogs. I heard them barking and knew they were close, turned off my hearing aid and prepared for attack. There were three of them, ferociously barking and snapping. Quick movements with my formidable stick and all three dogs are scampering off back towards the farm with a reassuring yelp. The very next morning, watching down from my high point up the mountains, I could see the expats walking their dogs and encountering no problems from the farm. A couple noticed me perched up on the cliff and waved thanks. I would stay up here and be introduced to Pepe, the local goat shepherd. He was weathered with this hot sun and an excellent slingshot of which he taught me the technique. One night, up in the mountains exploring, I was suddenly surrounded by a herd of goats, all looking so splendid and majestic. It was an honour to be surrounded by nudging goats and I admiringly watched them clamber further up the mountain aided by the slingshot diversionary tactics led by Pepe. I thought everything was fine but if only people would leave me alone. My girlfriend's parents were becoming concerned at my behaviour and wanting to ensure my wellbeing. I refused to come down and plotted out my ground up there in those wonderful mountains with the twinkling glamour of Puerto Banus below and the glimmering lights on the North African shoreline.

The land belongs to the people of Spain. They made my heart sing and made me feel alive. It is a place where I'd happily instil a door and call it home. I was doing stuff with the Spanish farmers which I enjoyed, while others thought I was being irrational. I still hid in the mountains, then one night had a personal light show where I'd projected myself onto the face of the cliff. I was a giant in the mountain but this action attracted others to come see what was up there. A jeep was coming up fast so I had to act quickly. The jeep approached and there were two young Spaniards sitting in it. They asked me questions in Spanish but it was pitch black up there in the mountains so after a few moments of silence a rock suddenly bounced off the floor then another. That was enough for these guys who promptly wheelspun, shooting back down the mountain. Damn Pepe, what a slingshot you are, but thanks for this. The next morning I went back down to the village and slept in the Arabic guy's garden.

When I woke there were two Spanish paramedics about to administer CPR on me. I managed to fob them off before they fired the electrical pulse. Good timing too! After a little arguing I convinced them I was fine and would make my way home. I went back to collect my things and cadged a lift to the airport. Unfortunately, at Malaga Airport it was the height of the summer season and there were no flights available back to the UK. I was persuaded to come back to the villa, preferring to sleep at the airport rather than have further disagreements. As we got back to the villa a disagreement ensued and I buggered off up the mountains to seek my solace and peace.
The next morning I could see a few people coming up the mountains so I hid out. I gave up when I saw a Search and Seek plane flying over looking for me. In some ways I took over the mountains. I set up a road block. I was in the process of cleaning up the mountains, recycling any found rubbish. Clearly I was home here; the mountain is in my heart. When the plane flew over, I acknowledged it as one knows one's limits especially when authority gets involved. I came back down to the villa and was put in a car

with Bert, a doctor who lived on the estate. Arabic and the Canadian sat in the back with me and said I needed to be assessed because I had spent so long in the mountains that people were concerned for my wellbeing. We went on a long road trip and they allowed me to smoke so I didn't mind. I knew we were headed somewhere no good and my fears were confirmed when we arrived at the hospital. I tried jumping out of the car but Arabic and the Canadian held me secure while the South African drove faster. I love these escapes as I get to meet many interesting people along the way.

We got to the hospital and I was put into a consulting room. A stern-looking Spanish speaking doctor came in and enquired whether my companions were family or not. On denial, they all left the room and I felt so alone again. I don't blame these guys as they were only doing their best for me. I don't know when I'm behaving dangerously or lucidly, but when there is joy then that's the feeling I'll keep in my heart. That gets me through a lot of dark moments. This was one of them. Goodbye, fellas! We'll meet again!

Suddenly six security guards shot into the room, all with pistols and pointed very directly at me. Before I could react, I stood still knowing that I could brook no argument with six mean-looking pistols facing me. It's a sight that stays with me and still does. I was gestured to lie on a trolley bed where I was immediately strapped down and injected. Blackout times again.

I awoke and was in some recovery room. Post-op recovery room? Shit, what've they done? I sensed my body and there was no pain. I was still strapped to a gurney. A water bottle was provided with plastic tubing. I managed to get a nurse's attention but they were all Spanish. Nobody understood English. My hearing aids had been taken away. Nobody knew anything. I was angry and became argumentative. I could only drop my water bottle to the floor in anger, being restrained and injected again. Huh-oh, these blackout rides are weird. You feel sensations of being moved (which you are) but you're so detached from your body. Your senses feel everything that is going on but it all has no rationale. Senseless, detached and far removed from wherever I was. I had no idea how much time had passed but again I awoke, clad in light green pyjamas with the logos of 'Hospital Clinico Universitario Virgen de la Victoria' emblazoned across my back, my left sleeve and left trouser leg. Oh, to be in this senseless place. This time I was strapped into a wheelchair, being wheeled down endless corridors and lifts, nothing made any sense in any direction. The corridors were all the same but devoid of people. We suddenly stopped at some serious steel doors with a hatch. A face opened it and peered out, looking at me for some time and uttering Spanish. The hatch closed then the doors opened slowly and there was another serious-looking door. Where was this place? I was dreading what was to come. Spanish? Hmm, let's see how far we can go.

The door behind me clanged shut and was locked with a resounding thud on the bolts. The second door opened revealing a long corridor devoid of any feeling. I was wheeled in and released. The first thing to do before I get out of here is to ask for my hearing aids back. No fucker's keeping them as they help me feel secure in this noisy world. Machines and spoken language, collaborating to drown out our screams.

Immediately I realised nobody spoke English. I was definitely locked up in a

Spanish psychiatric ward. It didn't take long to meet the other inmates, a mixed ward and every one of them wearing the same pyjamas with logos. This was serious shit! I felt heavy, sluggish and sat on a wooden bench. Again it was clear that cigarettes are the currency. It was hard to think, to try and talk. The language was all in Spanish and my knowledge of this was limited. I couldn't hear anything as no one had any idea what I was jabbering about concerning my hearing aids so clearly someone had swiped them. I was feeling so heavy-headed and wasn't able to lift my chin. I was dribbling in a drugged stupor and there was nothing else I could do. No one on the ward paid attention to this – seeing it as part and parcel of psychiatric ward life. Soon we were ushered into a queue for afternoon tea. We were given a milky substance and a bread roll. No butter here but olive oil sachets.

Being new here, I was wary as fuck but so sluggish. It was a struggle to walk. I sat watching the others and noticed they imbibed everything quickly and soon saw why. One inmate refused her drink resulting in the nursing staff banging her head on the table and making her drink it. They weren't afraid to be physical considering the violent tendencies of some patients, taking no nonsense from anyone on the ward and a tough regime. What is this place, I wondered, in my stupor of darkness? Where am I? Where is help? I had no idea where I was and no idea how long I was to be here. There was no communication. Zilch. Nothing. 'Viva España!' I sang in my mind.

After the tea break was over we were ushered out to a courtyard surrounded by walls about eight metres high topped with razor wire. Fuck, I thought, is this prison?

There was a large grassy area with a shaded area at the rear. Sun loungers are quickly grabbed or you sit on the floor if you're not quick enough. There's no view to see except the outside of the hospital building and the endless beautiful blue skies of Spain. One wasn't allowed to sit in the sun for more than ten minutes, so by the end of this leisure time we all were sitting in the shaded area avoiding eye contact with the nursing staff. Cigarettes and Spanish conversations are the norm here so my wariness eased a bit. I didn't know where I was sleeping so I was waiting and alert to any incidents. Everything was heavy and slow. I was drugged, but how? When would I get to go home? There was no information whatsoever.

It wasn't long before the regime schedule kicked in and we were ushered back inside from the courtyard. We had to queue and this time for the evening meal. You don't get to mess about in this ward, the staff are more aggressive but then the patients on the ward were quite wappy. I couldn't make much sense being in this drugged stupor so when I got a plate of ham and a bread roll I asked for the vegetarian version and this resulted in my head being pounced on the table and being made to eat ham. A lesson learnt there quickly. I'm in some serious place and I don't know where. Nobody has been in contact and I still have no idea what is happening. The cutlery is all plastic and paper plates. The staff are constantly supervising, leaving you on edge as they made sure you eat every morsel of food given. In the evenings the others would either pace up and down the corridor or sit and smoke in the TV room. Television on that Spanish psychiatric ward is constantly on either Game Show or Bullfighting. Visitors would come during the evenings, bringing supplies of cigarettes, but it was astounding for me to observe how Spanish families were more open on the subject of mental health. Their posture and mannerism suggested a break from the humdrum of everyday life. They were more positive in their dialogue with their related patient, who could be seriously fucked on drugs, and they still cared for them. I've never seen a whole room filled with families so accepting of mental health. Soon it was time to queue up for the evening drink and no one was allowed to neglect this routine. We all queued up and were given our drinks. It was a weird milky drink substance that neither tasted of tea nor coffee. Soon we were ordered to bed and I was back to being wary even though this stupor made everything slow for me.

On entering the bedroom with two other male patients, with three single beds all facing the door, I was assigned the middle bed so I knew now I would have hassle from both sides. They clanked the door shut and it was sleep time. I waited for the fuckers next to me to ambush me, to attack me or, even worse, assault me sexually. These were serious patients in here. I waited and waited, waiting all night long for the attack. Dawn rose and I realised I was going to be safe here. Nobody fucks with this system. I had lain awake all night waiting for this ambush, but not only that, I was thinking about my dire current situation. I was sleepy and just about to nod off around five in the morning when I was ambushed. It was the nursing team and they restrained me and stabbed my belly with a needle. This was how they were drugging me. It continued every day during my stay there and I could never beat those bastards by waiting for them because they always got me. Damn smart nurses!

In the mornings the staff would jolt us awake and we had to strip ourselves of our pyjamas and queue for the shower. Everyone was naked but didn't mess around, especially with the nursing staff ordering us around. Later, after breakfast, I was sat on the bench, falling into that stupor of sluggishness and slowly falling to the floor. Another patient came over and eased me back up, putting a cigarette in my mouth and instructing me to inhale. We struck up a friendship and he was quite lively on the ward. In my stupor we came to an understanding to gather as many cigarettes as we could so that we could share them in the evenings. The others on the ward got to know me and I was 'the English', to them. I got used to this drugged routine, eating when ordered to, showering when being told, and exchanging pyjamas daily with that same emblazoned logo. It took a while to go for a shit as there were no doors. You just shit and that's it. I worked out outdoor leisure time was the best as no one would bother me having a shit as they would if we all were on the ward. I felt part of them and felt more at ease despite not knowing any information about my status in this crazy asylum.

Days passed by, an endless repeat of the regime. Up, shower and breakfast then leisure time. Lunch and leisure time followed by the evening meal and visitors' times. It was lovely sitting in the gardens during leisure time. We would all be scattered everywhere with our sun loungers, sitting it out in this glorious Spanish sunshine. We smoked and sometimes chatted. There was always a bout of violence kicking off but this was quickly repressed by the formidable nursing staff. I was starting to become used to this new drug, still being ambushed in the mornings with that syringe, falling into stupor. Cigarettes were my comfort at this time and I became adept at asking for cigarettes in fluent Spanish. Some families who were visiting had come to know me, sometimes bringing sweets or chocolate which I shared with my ward buddy.

A friend turned up out of the blue but didn't bring any cigarettes, just news that a plane ticket was being arranged and I was to go back to the UK. No news, no message and absolutely nothing else. Great – fucking considerate! I went back to my routine of indoors and outdoors, forgetting about time. Through my conversations with the other inmates, I learned a lot of Spanish and about my communication issues with practically everyone. I don't understand why people feel they have the right to intervene when I say to leave me alone. What business is it of others if I have made my own choices in life? I was dealing with issues of my deafness, my identity crisis, and finding comfort in their conversations. Despite the everyday violence, this place was becoming home. It was hardcore with its regime; everything was done to a function and strictly on time. Absolutely no messing about at this place unless you want a confrontation with the staff and there were plenty of those.

I laid in the hot, scorching sunshine when a shadow crossed my face. It was the Spaniard. He came to warn me that the nursing staff were calling me. I looked up and all the other patients were pointing at me. I looked at the nurse who was gesturing angrily at me to come and follow him. I was dismayed as I wasn't sure why and I didn't like him as he was aggressive to the patients. I got up and walked towards him while he was still gesturing away. It twigged! My plane ticket was ready to take me home. As I followed the nurse back into the ward, I looked at my fellow compatriots and waved. A second passed, and they all smiled and waved back at me. This was a very moving moment because they had become my friends and now I would never see them again. I went back on the ward and was stripped of my pyjamas and given my clothes back. These were still dusty from my escape up the mountains so I had a familiar sense of smell. They unlocked the doors and escorted me to reception where I was to collect my passport. Some aggravation ensued as they insisted on my showing them my passport before they could open the safe. Thanks to the Spanish I learnt on the ward I was able to relay to them that my passport is in the bloody safe! I left escorted to the airport by some friends feeling exhilarated and somewhat surreal after being in that damned place for so long.

I landed at Manchester Airport and came out to find my concerned parents waiting for me. They looked me straight in the eye and asked if I was alright. I beamed and grinned that I was fine and they were relieved to find me as myself. We headed back to Sheffield and I was happy to be back in my bedsit but not for long because I decided to move to London. I was seeing a number of psychiatrists at this time but rejected all of them until I came across a Spanish psychiatrist. I had a brief conversation with him speaking Spanish and we were able to establish our trust and resume a routine of psychiatric assessments. Time passed quickly and I moved to London.

6. The Lure of London

I had a room in a shared house in Elephant and Castle, sharing with three other men. London was too much for me and I was realising that this new medication the Spaniards had given me was still affecting me. It would take at least three to six months before the medicine could stabilise my moods and with the dosage I was given I was becoming more lethargic. The busyness of London assaulted my senses and I found myself preferring to explore the city in the late hours of the night. I was becoming isolated with the others in the house but only because my depression had come back and that sinking feeling reappeared. It wasn't so comfortable adjusting to the side effects of the medication and this impounded on my mental stability. I started to sleep during the days, preferring to miss all the traffic, then wake late in the evenings, cook a meal and go out roaming the streets through the darkness. I met so many weird people, creatures of the night, had amazing conversations with them. I saw a lot of violence on the streets, mainly gangster activities in their expensive cars. I went to the easyCafe so I could engage with the world through emails and conduct my business. I enjoyed

London but only at night-time. I would roam round central London, exploring the City, the riverfront and all the usual tourist trappings. Trafalgar Square is amazing at three thirty in the morning. The tranquil ambience of this amazing city that is a constant hive, of Piccadilly Circus with the deadbeat crowd. There was always somewhere to explore as it was better than being at home. I was sinking into a deep depression again and hated being here. I must've driven the guys in the house mad but they were good enough to let me be.

Once I came back from a night's exploration I went to see the doctors and somehow ended with double rations of prescription drugs, went home and took them all in one go. I lay on my bed, contorting with the physical pain of the impending overdose. I had had enough. Everything has its time and place, its procedures and routine. The buses start early here, carrying the increasing throng of money-hungry workers. The tube is packed and I avoided this, preferring to walk. My consciousness was fading and then it was over. Blackout time.
Sudden impulsive suicide attempts are not me as I was later to realise. I am a determined person and will carry through plans. Unfortunately for me, an

early death is part of my plan. I don't understand this feeling, but sinking into that depression is tough and despair overtook. I wasn't sure how long I was out for. I woke, still in my bed, and walked into the living room where my housemates were watching a game, cheering that I had finally woken. I had been asleep for four days while my body filtered this poison in my system. Nobody knew of this and I kept it to myself knowing yet again I had denied death. I continued falling into the blackness, the depression pulling me down with defiance. Around this time my lease was up so I moved back to Sheffield.

I continued to see the Spanish psychiatrist, visiting as an outpatient at regular intervals that decreased over time. I was doing reasonably well and was able to rationalise everything into place. I was under his supervision for seven years before being discharged. My night habits stayed with me and it took me three months to re-adapt to living during the day. Sheffield is much more laid-back with plenty of countryside nearby and I enjoyed walking so got a dog. My dog was a special dog as he was my guide dog. Without him I would not be where I am. My mood improved and I was more stabilised now that the medication had had six months to settle. I was raring to go back to work and did so until one fateful afternoon in February 2015.

7. The River Thames Calls Me

I'm not sure what happened on that February day but it was the first time I had called in sick at work. I suppose it was a maelstrom of middle age crisis, career crisis, financial crisis and relationship crisis. Everything went into meltdown that day. In the previous two years I had to rebuild my life after a relationship went sour. During this time I started smoking legal highs, otherwise known as spice. This is fake cannabis and I couldn't believe I could walk into a shop and walk out smoking it. Over those two years I had developed a dependency on it and was smoking it every day especially after I finished work. I would wander these mean streets of London in a daze and enjoy all the sensations that this spice was inducing in me. Looking back, it was a mistake, because in the end all drugs fuck you up one way or other.

My life was a constant question of "What is the meaning of life?" I couldn't find an answer despite talking to lots of people who led amazing lives in London. I was dismayed that as I turned to 45 years of age that there was nothing but a rented flat and a car to show for all my efforts. I really loved my job and enjoyed every aspect of it but inside I was yearning for something else. My finances were in a poor state because I owed monies to Inland Revenue and being hooked onto spice was a costly habit to have. I questioned my own qualities because it seemed that every relationship I had failed. Maybe my standards were too rigid or I was too carefree; I wasn't sure but right now, at this moment, I am worth nothing to anybody.

That day I took off sick I tried to sort out my finances but it was clear I had a problem here. I had become hooked on spice not realising the consequences of such dangerous drugs. It had become my crutch but right now I had had enough of everything. I decided to go for a walk along the banks of the River Thames near where I lived and see if some fresh air could help me think more clearly. I don't remember much at the flat except locking the door when I left. I walked along the River Thames and it was a beautiful day. The seabirds were soaring and hovering over me which made me smile at their simplicity of life. I'm not sure how time passed because it was falling dark quite quickly on this cold February day. I walked on and reached a viewing platform and went up to think and try to resolve my issues. I observed the river going out with its tide and it's a mighty river that garners my admiration, reminding me of the River Humber. The tide went down revealing the muddy banks and a pile of broken paving slabs that vandals had uplifted and thrown in.

I was mesmerised by this scene, drawn by the constant squawking of those lovely seabirds. The tide had dropped to its very low level and now I was looking at this riverbed from a considerable height. Everything was crystal clear, I wasn't befuddled and I took pleasure from the company of these seabirds. It only took four seconds to make a crazy decision. For some reason I challenged myself to stand on the wall, on the edge of the parapet, looking down at a jump of some twenty-five metres. The wind was cold and the stars witness to this spectacle. I stood looking down when my mind screamed "Jump," and followed by "Get down!".

This went on for four long seconds; it was only four seconds because I wanted to get to ten and get down and quit this foolish game. Everything in my mind flared up, all the problems I was having tumbling in freefall into my mind. On the fourth second, I'd had enough and I jumped.

The fall was so peaceful and serene, everything a warm haze of blackness. I could feel coldness somewhere but right now it was so beautiful having this feeling of peace. "Open your eyes", something screamed in me, "Open your eyes!!" it was now shouting. I was confused. Where was I? Is this how the end looks? A plethora of darkness in different hues. The shouting in my head was getting louder and louder that I had no choice but to open my eyes, and thud! I was in a daze unsure where I was, then I looked up and saw the imposing viewing platform I had jumped from. Fuck, fuck, fuck, I cursed, realising I was still alive. I can't die! I passed out immediately only for the tide to turn and wash over me with its cold freezing waters and I jolted awake again. My survival instincts kicked in as this tide was frighteningly fast and was already covering my head. I tried to stand up but collapsed realising I had broken both feet. I had landed on that pile of vandalised paving slabs. I crawled through the mud and saw the quayside ladders in front of me; it was a formidable climb because I could only use my arms to get out. I heaved myself through this slimy, cold mud and started pulling myself up. I didn't think about anything except to go rung after rung up the ladder. My back was in pain but that was the least of my worries right now. As I got to the top I had to grab a fence in order to get over it, but it was a metre away from the ladders and I could only lunge to grab it. I had one opportunity to do this otherwise I was going way back down to the riverbed. One jump is enough and it's definitely not recommended.

With a deep breath I lunged for the fence and grabbed a railing, then with strength from somewhere I managed to hurl myself over the fence falling onto the ground. I was hyperventilating and freezing cold and wet. The wind was blowing and I seriously thought I'd completely fucked myself up even worse. I lay there on the ground trying to control my breathing and thought fuck it, there's no one around and I can't walk. I decided to let hypothermia finish me off so I closed my eyes and waited. Twenty minutes later my hyperventilating had calmed and I was freezing cold; I realised that I wasn't going to die. The way I could sort out this stupidity was to sort it out myself. I tried to stand up holding the fence but my feet were completely gone and useless. There were no flats or houses around, the nearest being a twenty-minute walk away. I started crawling on all fours, one hand, one knee, other hand then other knee. It was very painful and the pain in my back was certainly feeling very uncomfortable. One by one I crawled, shouting for help, but there was no one apart from three foxes watching me with interest.

I crawled and crawled. There was no other option. I decided to try reaching the nearest block of flats and calling for help there. After long a while I got there. I really wished I could phone but it got soaked in the river and I couldn't have a smoke either! I got to the flats and started yelling for help but no one responded. I could see people in their flats but they were all engrossed in their televisions. Hmm, perhaps death is merciless and will punish those who attempt a premature exit. I was thinking about my predicament and kind of going into a maniacal laughter as I couldn't believe I had jumped so far and survived. It's the worse decision I have ever made but I couldn't think about that right now. I crawled further towards the main road where I knew the twenty-four hour buses ran. I saw someone walking up the path and they were shocked to see me and another couple came; together they called for the emergency services. They were from abroad, possibly Eastern Europe, as I couldn't tell what they were saying. My hearing aids had broken too.

They kept me company while I crouched on all fours because my back was really hurting.

Eventually, an emergency response paramedic turned up in his car and promptly told me to get in the back of the car. I was in agony by then and I figured he thought I was some drunk or a tramp. After all, I was covered in the glorious Thames mud and did not look normal to those who saw me that night. I wanted to kill the paramedic – he was a complete shit. He kept telling me to turn around and sit normally in the back seat of the car. I struggled as my feet couldn't do anything and my back was screaming, turning around to face him only to find he was useless at communicating. No matter how many times I told him I was deaf, he kept talking to me while facing the windscreen. Luckily, an ambulance came and two more paramedics pulled me out of the car and made me walk with these useless feet to the back of the ambulance. They were uncertain what was wrong with me so I stripped off and when they saw my feet they scrambled into action. I was laid on the gurney and demanded oxygen while they radioed around for which hospital to take me to. I was warned it was going to be a long journey, but inhaling the oxygen cleared my head and I fell asleep. I managed to catch the time off the paramedic's watch and realised I had been crawling on my hands and knees for five and half hours. The things one does for survival!

I woke when we arrived and was wheeled into King's College Hospital, being taken to the emergency room. I don't remember much except having to be vocally aggressive in letting the medical team know I was deaf. It really is an invisible disability and no one thinks of the dangers miscommunication can cause. I was to have an operation immediately and be left in the care of the emergency team so everything from here is spent unconsciously. I vaguely remember signing the consent form for a spinal operation and the surgeon warning me that I could be paralysed. Karma indeed! I woke on a ward and couldn't move. My head was spinning due to the morphine administered. Everything is a blend of blurred reality and broken dreams.I am not sure what is real except this pain I have inflicted on myself. I could see my right leg was winched up with some hefty scaffolding screwed into it. My left was covered in plaster. I had a metal plate fitted on my spine and had a total of three operations, one on my spine and the other two on my feet.

I see my family come and go in a blurred sense of unreality. Nothing made sense except the doctors and nurses who came and went. Recovery was painful and I couldn't really move. I had a catheter inserted which was a pain but at least I could pee. I drifted in and out of consciousness, affected by the morphine. Each day I would attempt to raise myself by using the electric recliner on the bed, doing it bit by bit as it was so painful. Eventually I could sit up enough to be able to eat and take a look at my legs. My sister visited me on a regular basis, providing moral support and dealing with my finances that were a train wreck. One morning I was given a wheelchair so I was able to get into the bathroom to clean myself up. I looked at the mirror and stood up, promptly falling onto the floor. I pressed the alarm and was rescued by the nursing staff who queried what I was doing. I only wanted to shave and it hit me then that life in a wheelchair was going to be a difficult adjustment. Everything is designed for people standing up. I was given a board so I could transfer myself from my bed to my wheelchair and then onto the toilet. Life was very interesting from that perspective.

One night I was tripping because of the morphine. I'm uncertain how but I found myself by the hospital window, peering out into the darkness. How I got there I have no idea but I was deluded because I thought I was in Paris. I'd broken into someone's house and was creeping around this place. I noticed my catheter and pulled it out of my penis spilling blood across the floor. It was then that the nursing staff came into the ward and noticed me by the window. They put me back to bed and the next morning, in a haze, I had the catheter reinserted. Another couple of nights later, I was on the edge of my mind. I was annoyed by the constant flicker of the morphine feeding machine. It would beep every time I applied an extra dose of morphine but it must have sent my mind racing away because the next thing I knew I was arguing with the nursing staff, demanding a wheelchair so I could go home. I wasn't very pleasant that night but I didn't want to be there. In my confrontation with the nursing staff I ended arguing with a psychiatrist with my sister listening to all this via FaceTime. It was a tense situation because I was disturbing the other patients on the ward and ended with sixteen nursing staff and three security guards pinning me down to my bed. I had to be sedated and fell asleep. The next morning the ward was evacuated and there were only the three security guards who were staring at me with such hostility that it wasn't long before we had a disagreement and one of them was punching my face. What a wanker.

I was moved to another ward and was given twenty-four hour supervision by mental health nurses. I was not to be left alone. It was annoying because they just sat there watching everything I did and would often try to come in the bathroom with me when I needed a shit. Three shifts a day they would sit there, but the guy on the night shift was really great and I got on very well with him. I was also being visited by a psychiatrist from the Maudsley Hospital who warned me that if I attempted suicide again and survived I would be put into a high security psychiatric ward for life. These were harsh words but a fact and it was something that would remain in my mind for a long time. Due to my being in a wheelchair, and being deaf, it was deemed that I would be at risk from the other inmates so it was being arranged, through my family, for me to attend a deaf psychiatric hospital in Tooting. This was the National Deaf Services at St George's Mental Health NHS Trust known as the Springfield Hospital. My sister and my mother went to visit to see if it would be suitable for me and they returned with beaming smiles saying I'd love it there. There is a ward for deaf patients called the Bluebell Ward and this would be where I was to go. I was a little hesitant because I'd never been in a deaf mental health unit and wasn't sure what to expect. I was in this blasted wheelchair but it would be great to get out of here.

My transfer to the Bluebell was delayed because of an infection on my ankle so I was put on antibiotics which was hell but necessary. After five long weeks of staying at the King's College Hospital I was deemed fit and ready to move. I have to thank the nursing team and doctors there because they really did look after me despite my difficulty. I felt so much better once the morphine was stopped and my rage ceased. The ambulance came and I was wheeled into the back and they drove me across London. It was wonderful to see the outside world again. As we arrived at Springfield Hospital I could see that it was an old psychiatric hospital, with beautiful grounds and buildings. I was wheeled into the building realising the ward was on the first floor so the staff sent me up in the lift. I was wheeled onto the ward seeing around nine patients huddled round signing away. I was waiting for the first bout of violence to erupt but nothing. Just a friendly hello from them all and an offer of a cup of tea. The nursing staff all used sign language and I was shown to my room. I had the disabled room because of my wheelchair and, after having travelled across London to get here, my back was aching with pain. I lay on my bed and watched a lovely sunset with parakeets zipping across outside my window. After a little sleep I ventured out and the other patients started asking me questions, asking about why I was in a wheelchair. It was weird because usually by now something has kicked off or someone is being aggressive but here everyone was so friendly that I was wary. It made such a change for me because I was able to relax, able to sign in conversation and even sign with the nurses. I couldn't believe the difference that this place had on me simply because the communication is all in sign language. Even the following morning when I woke up I wheeled myself out of my room to be confronted by a nursing staff signing "Good morning" to me that I had to go back into my room and come out again just to be sure that I had really seen this spectacle.

After seeing the ward psychiatrist and meeting the nursing team responsible for me I was put on a programme of activities and recovery. I was to have sixteen sessions of Cognitive Analysis Therapy (CAT) with gym sessions twice a week to try getting me back on my feet. There was an Occupational Therapist who ran a programme during the week so it was a hive of busyness there. I got to know the other patients on the ward and would often chat away about everything. I did cry a lot during this time because I came to accept that I had tried to kill myself. I had destroyed my feet and broken my back. I was reckless in this stupid decision to jump into the River Thames. It took a while for me to accept that I could be dangerous to myself, and with the CAT sessions I was able to understand myself better and understand the reasons why I behaved as I did that night. It helped me to understand why I had committed so many suicide attempts and for the first time in twenty-three years, I had a better understanding of myself and my own logic. The physiotherapist was really good as she got me working out on all the gym equipment in her attempt to get me walking again. I couldn't have achieved the simple feat of standing up unsupported without her help. It was after about nine weeks of gym training and visits back to the King's College Hospital to see the surgeon for his final approval before I stood up independently. I want to describe that moment because I was overwhelmed with emotions when I achieved this feat, and soon I would be walking with the aid of crutches; but it was a slow process but worth every minute of determination.

After eleven weeks on the Bluebell Ward I was deemed fit to leave the hospital and go into temporary accommodation. I couldn't go back to my flat because it was on the first floor so I was to live in Erith which I'd never heard of. I got to my new place which was nice enough and realised that this was it – I was alone again. I had to hobble on crutches to the supermarket and hobble back home. It was a painful journey to make but essential if I was to remain independent. I even went back to work, struggling on crutches in the madness of London's rush hour commute. It was strange being alone after the Bluebell Ward as I missed all the camaraderie. It took me a while to get used to this but work was a struggle for me because I realised that I couldn't commit myself to it fully. I needed more time to recover and rediscover my pleasures of life. I continued to see the psychologist for my CAT sessions but this soon came to an end with my having a greater understanding of my mind. The psychiatrist there warned me that I had a 'trigger-happy death switch' by which I am capable of committing suicide promptly. There's no guarantee it won't happen again, hence keeping in touch with the Deaf Adult Community Team (DACT) and with my local Community Mental Health Team (CMHT). I am also now in constant contact with my family especially my sisters, so if there are any warning bells in my head then I have my support network to contact immediately.

Life has changed dramatically, having built up the strength to walk with crutches. I still find it difficult to walk distances or without having a rest but walk I can, and walk I will. I now have another job and continually write my thoughts as this is very therapeutic for me. I have taken to doing presentations and performing my written pieces as a way of raising awareness of the work that the Bluebell Ward does. It's become so important to me because the simple fact of communicating in British Sign Language made a big difference to my recovery. Had I been put onto another hearing mainstream psychiatric ward I don't think I would have recovered as well as I have today.

Now I am still a mean motherfucker but only in my mind. I keep my mouth shut and just get on with participating in everyday society. Life is beautiful and too precious to waste. I feel in some ways ashamed of what I have done to myself but that's mental health for you. It's a dark place to be in when you're down and an exciting place to be when you're on a high. My mania is more controlled with the help of my medication, thanks to the Spanish psychiatric system. I'm much more stable and calm, which is a massive improvement to the mood swings I suffered.

Life goes on and we all try our best so I walk these streets of London, relishing every moment of freedom I have. I appreciate that I will never be able to run again due to my feet being shattered but I'm grateful that I can walk. It's with gratitude and appreciation to all the nursing teams involved in my care because all they want is for you to be at your best. I must extend a special thanks to the Bluebell Ward because they are the people who saved me in the end.

Night is falling so I shall take a walk to chat with the stars.